To Silvia, Eddie and Benji.
Here's something to eat.
Simon

To all my main bitches.
You know who you are.
Yumi

THE FOOD FIX

Real World
Dinner
Solutions for
The Exhausted

Yumi Stynes   **Simon Davis**

murdoch books
Sydney | London

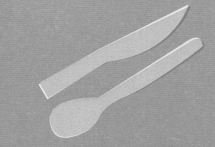

CONTENTS

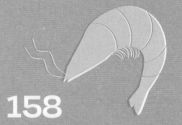

WELCOME TO THE FOOD FIX

This is not one of those cookbooks you'll leaf through, sighing wistfully at a bunch of photogenic but ultimately unachievable dishes that you would cook if only you had a personal assistant, futuristic gadgetry, the spare time of a celibate retiree and your own personal dishwashing kid. If you know our podcast (from which these pages have been expertly baked), then you'll understand that the two of us are here to put big food wins squarely within the reach of the everyday home cook. Because great food should be for everyone, right? Especially those of us who love eating and love food, but want to create it free from snobbery and unrealistic expectations – and possibly do it while a small child is clinging to one's leg like a koala to a tree.

This book has been years in the making. We've tested every recipe multiple times, we've tried them on our mercilessly honest families and, like pigs hunting truffles, we've sought the shortcuts. We've found the easy ways to spin the crap in your pantry into culinary gold. We share a relentless enthusiasm for, and curiosity about, food. And not to brag (although, hey ... we will), we both have a pretty honed and expert sense of what tastes good, and what is nonsense!

There are no *MasterChef*-style culinary pyrotechnics, inedible superfoods or trendy ingredients that are impossible to find, and no TikTok fads that sound great and taste garbage. Those things all have a time and a place, but that place is elsewhere. What you'll find here is a treasure trove of unexpected ideas: simple, honest recipes; clever hacks; and meals that you'll find yourself cooking over and over until you're well into your old age (when you're a sexy, non-celibate retiree, hopefully).

We're busy. We're tired. Oh god, we're hungry now, too! We need food that suits the way we lead our lives. If we achieve what we set out to do with this book, then every page will deliver an opportunity for you to cook something that will have people saying, 'Wow! This is so delicious, how did you do it?' and – crucially – you'll be able to answer, 'You won't believe how easy it was.'

Too Busy? Too Expensive? Don't Know How?

We all make a lot of excuses about why we can't or won't cook. And while we can agree that most of us are busy, burnt out and deeply exhausted, we can hopefully also agree that making food is a satisfying way to be creative and nurturing – to your own tired self as well as your loved ones, on a daily basis.

No matter who you are, you still gotta eat, and it's better to eat well. It pains me gravely to see young people on minimum wage working their asses off only to spend a huge proportion of their income on home food delivery. While it's a luxurious feeling of reward to have cooked food dropped at your door, if you make it yourself it WILL be better in terms of a) cost (obviously), b) food quality, and c) use of disposable packaging.

Yes, we're busy, but we can make efficient use of our kitchen time with a tiny bit of planning, foresight and competence. This is why the recipes in this book are easy and low-intervention, with a lot of set and forget.

Simon and I live in the real world and each of us has a family to support. Cost is always a consideration – for this book and in our lives.

Neither of us eats a lot of meat. When we do, we don't tend to go for the expensive kind – we like using tasty, nutritious (and usually cheaper) cuts. And speaking of cost, I love having plans for leftovers. Because at work or school, a lunch from home is almost always yummier than a bought one, and definitely always cheaper!

If you're thinking 'But I'm a terrible cook', I have a lot of fun remembering what a rotten cook I was aged 19. I made instant ramen noodles (badly) and had a pie-making machine that I filled with creamed corn and tinned tuna. I also ate a lot of toast. And once in a while I cooked a semi-edible pasta. But I quite liked a vegetable stir-fry, and gradually started to figure out how to make the stir-fry better, what worked and what led to failure. And through that tiny little window of competence, I squeezed in and started to learn and build on what I knew. What we want to do here is equip you with new ways to be competent. None of them is hard, a lot of them are common sense, but unless you had a friend or a parent at your elbow while you were cooking as a youngster, you might have missed out on learning them. Please imagine us as the friend at your elbow.

Dealing with the Dreaded 'What's for Dinner?'

It would help if loved ones said, 'Hey, I love that delicious XYZ thing that you do, could we have that for dinner tomorrow?' That kind of feedback is a form of incidental decision-making and, to most cooks, is extremely welcome. Tragically, in our experience, those requests are extremely rare.

Here's the thing. If a decision about what's for dinner has to be made – and it does – then you need to take charge. You're taking feedback, but you're not taking orders.

You, my friend, are running a kitchen autocracy. You're the boss! Take the agony out of the dreaded daily puzzle by remembering you are the one who has to solve it. Make a decision. (With love, obviously.) Decide what's for dinner based on what you have available (ingredients, but also time), what in your fridge urgently needs to be used, and of course everyone's dietary preferences. And then? No argument shall be entered into unless some other idiot wants to cook!

Hot tip: the earlier in the day you make the decision, the better you'll feel. You won't be puzzling over what to cook, and you'll know whether or not you need to pick up a tin of chickpeas on the way home. Once you autocratically decide what's for dinner, you'll be more at ease, because the gnawing need to answer the burning question will have been replaced by purpose and an appreciation for the yumminess that lies ahead.

Try taking a photo of the contents of your fridge in the morning so you remember what's in there while you're at the shops like a zombie clutching a shopping list with a head empty of everything but deadlines and despair ... If it helps you to feel less bonkers, I also have dozens of photos in my phone of where I parked my car, because who can remember this stuff?!

So you autocratically decide what's for dinner.

Good.

As dictator you may wish to announce your decision to your subjects, or you may wish to keep it to yourself. It's up to you, King.

Easy Wins = Wins!

**W**e've established that you're king of your kitchen/lord of the larder/queen of your own home cooking scene (delete as applicable) and you now know that you have to be the one making the decisions. But where do you start?

Remember this – there's nothing wrong with easy wins. Too often in the kitchen, as in life, 'perfect' gets in the way of good. And that's when the problems set in. Because if you set the bar impossibly high, you're only going to be disappointed when you fail to meet those lofty (and unrealistic) expectations.

Say your kids like to eat frozen peas from the bowl (as mine do). Then from time to time let them. If the alternative is coaxing, wheedling, bribing and extorting them into trying something else, say the adults' sautéed tenderstem broccoli with olives and a sourdough crumb, and it's only going to end in misery for all concerned, then this is not a battle worth fighting. (Believe me, I've died on this hill before so you don't have to.)

In the kitchen, you need to weigh up each situation on its merits. Short of time because you're racing home from the beach? Grab that roast chicken from the supermarket and pull something together in seconds when you get back rather than trying to create a lengthy meal from scratch when you get through the door and everyone is tired. And hungry. And over it. (And take a look at page 106 if you're after inspiration for what to do with the leftovers.)

This may sound like incredibly obvious advice, but you'd be surprised how often we fall into the trap of not making the right food for the right circumstances, which is ultimately what eating well at home is all about.

Am I, by extension, suggesting you do away with 'proper' cooking all together? Not at all. There's pleasure to be had in a lengthy cook involving plenty of technique – when you have time to potter around by the stove at the weekend, for example. But without wanting to sound too Zen about it, remember that it's all a question of *balance*.

Treat Meal Planning Like You're Putting on a Show

I think of cooking as a form of theatre. Before the curtain goes up and that first spark of heat is applied to a pan, before your apron is donned and your props and ingredients are all out and standing by, ready for their starring moment – before ALL of that, there has been some planning.

Conceptualisation: The less crowded your fridge and pantry are, the easier it is to think through your meal options and make sense of what ingredients you have available. To conceptualise your show, don't be afraid to use up your resources. Empty your fridge to allow room for new inspiration. If you've only got two carrots and a bag of onions left, the decisions about what to make actually get easier.

Pre-production: Understanding what you need to buy *before* you head to the shops gives you a huge head start in a) choosing the right stuff, and b) reducing waste. Maybe your starring role will go to a piece of fish or a couple of perfect tomatoes? But if you get to the shops and the star turns out to be manky, too expensive or unavailable, you've allowed time for fixes. Support roles like sides of pickles can be made well ahead of time, will enhance the meal and are part of the flow of a low-waste, functioning kitchen. And as it is in theatre, spontaneity is welcome but wildly overrated. Plan ahead to do a big batch of, say, bolognese, so that half can go in the freezer for later. The glory of just having to reheat your sauce to provide a nourishing meal deserves a standing ovation. Dal and chicken stock are also wonderfully useful to have in the freezer. Desserts like Dulce de Leche (page 211) and Magical Milo Ice Cream (page 179) can be on permanent standby and, like a good understudy, play their part when required and don't go off when not.

The Big Show: Showing some reverence for the food before commencing eating is common across cultures. In Japan we say 'itadaki-masu!' before even touching our chopsticks. In Australian cafes, we take a photo and post it on Instagram. In both instances, a little ceremony enhances the experience. Food should be put together considering contrasting colours, textures and flavours. You wouldn't cast a show where every actor looks the same, would you?

The Season: There's nothing wrong with having a meal plan, or even a loose meal 'pattern'. Simon has sausages sliced into coins with flatbreads on a Monday, roast chook or a store-bought rotisserie chicken with Quick Italian Roast Potatoes (page 51) on Wednesday, and homemade pizzas (page 44) every Thursday. I try to get to the fishmongers most Thursdays and, depending on what looks good, the kids will get either crumbed snapper or sashimi that night, while the next night they'll be ready for their favourite pasta (Creamy Bacon Penne, page 144). These patterns are reliable enough that we don't have to think too hard to solve the question of what's for dinner.

Equipment Essentials

The idea that a new gadget will fix your kitchen woes or help you cook like a pro is a consumerist sales technique. A new 'thing' won't do the cooking for you; it will clutter your space and eventually become landfill. There's always a new fad, and fads come and go.

My advice is, the next time you're tempted to spend money on a fancy appliance, get a good saucepan instead. The costs are comparable and the pan will last longer! There's nothing better for your cooking than a **good saucepan** with a lid that fits.

You also need a **decent frying pan** – such as a cast-iron skillet that's solid and reliable and you can use for 20 years.

Sharp knife? Do it. They don't have to cost hundreds. Mine's a Japanese one from a Tokyo department store, from a company that's been making knives for more than 200 years. The weight and gauge of it fits my hand perfectly. It cost $80. I take it in for a sharpening every couple of months and feel like a total legend. (I always buy Japanese knives, but that may be because I'm biased.)

I use my trusty **kitchen scales** three or four times a day. I have marvellously perfect **measuring cups** that I got from a suburban op shop, and **measuring spoons** and a series of **metal bowls** that fit inside each other like Russian dolls. I use all of these things many times a day and they're all built to last for years.

I use an **electric mixer** and a **food processor**, and I use them often enough that they sit permanently on my bench. And while it may be deeply unfashionable, I also have a **microwave** that I use at least once a day – often just to reheat a cup of tea, but also to cook my son's broccoli (page 77) and revive a bowl of sweet adzuki beans (page 201) for a late-night snack.

I also regularly use a couple of **wooden chopping boards**, a **silicone spatula**, **metal tongs**, **chopsticks, measuring jugs,** a **pair of scissors**, **sticky tape** and many **elastic bands** – but look at all these things with a critical eye and be sure that you really need them. You might be surprised by what you can live without, and also how much more functional a space is when it's not cluttered.

Your Kitchen, Your Cooking, Your Way

A great joy for me is listening to podcasts, the radio or audio books while I'm cooking. Cooking is all hands and body, audio is all brains and ears. The two can exist in glorious, synchronous parallel. Sometimes I listen to TV shows (and glance up for a sex scene, a marauding monster or an emotional moment). I have a voice-activated smart home assistant in the kitchen and I can shout things like, 'Hey, play the new Sampa the Great song', 'Set a timer for 7 minutes', 'Play 5 Minute Food Fix', or other super-handy stuff like, 'Hey, how much does half a cup of olive oil weigh?'.

To make my kitchen space feel like mine, I have two key family photos – one on the windowsill, one on top of the microwave – both of me and my four kids. They remind me to check in with my values ... because nothing is more important to me than those woolly-haired wombles.

It's appealing to think there's a template you can apply to all kitchens, but as chef, you need to centre your own needs. Circle back to that autocrat idea and do what works for you. Once, when I'd just moved into a new place, a friend who was helping me unpack told me I was doing it wrong and that the coffee cups should be near

the plates and bowls. But I wanted the cups near the kettle, and for months afterwards, every time I got a mug down from above the kettle, I wondered, 'What was she thinking?' Her style and mine just aren't the same.

One thing I find nightmarish in a kitchen is an excess of plastic containers, none of which match. They're not useful in that state – it's shitty McClutter. My container collection is small and functional – everything sits with its lid, in a spot that I can reach easily and make sense of. If a piece has lost its Significant Other and you can't bear to part with it, use it as a saucer for your mini pots of herbs until it can be reunited with its other half or recycled.

Ancient tins of food aren't going to become more alluring with passing time. Ask yourself if you'd be prepared to eat it today, or dare to feed it to friends. If not, then maybe you should just get rid of it. Declutter. Free up space. I love to open my cupboards in the knowledge that everything I see is neat, organised and edible.

I recently gave away a set of steak knives that had been in the main cutlery drawer for the past year, despite the fact that in that time we had not once eaten steak. You don't need every thing and every gadget. You just need what you use.

Preparing for Nuclear War (aka the Art of Kitchen Cupboard Management)

Yumi once asked me, 'How many days would you and your family survive on the food in your pantry if you could never leave the house?' To be honest, my answer ended up being measured in months, not days. I never realised it, but it turns out that when it comes to food, I'm a bit of a doomsday prepper. Oh dear.

You see, I love, love, love a full larder or kitchen cupboard. I find a certain satisfaction in opening the door, seeing those jars neatly stacked up and knowing the range of possibilities that lie ahead, and I genuinely get anxious if I don't have at least half a dozen tins of chopped tomatoes in there at all times.

This hardwired need for squirrelling has led to missteps along the way (that online order of spelt flour during Covid lockdown #2 was a mistake), but I think it comes down to knowing that, whatever the circumstances, I will always be able to put something on the table for dinner. And when I'm busy, exhausted and have zero mental capacity yet still have to feed several starving little people, it's impossible to put a price on that peace of mind.

You might not be as far along the survivalist scale as me and that's absolutely fine (probably healthy, even), but know that if you've got the building blocks of deliciousness to hand at all times, then you're multiplying your options for dinner that night and making the planning, procuring and preparation of whatever meal you do opt for that much easier. And who wouldn't want that?

Here are the things both Yumi and I have in the cupboard, fridge and freezer at all times.

Cupboard

Dried pasta – long, short, the works

Rice – risotto, long-grain, sushi, sticky

Dried lentils – red, yellow and Puy

Tinned tomatoes

Tinned coconut milk and coconut cream

Tomato passata (puréed tomatoes)

Tinned pulses – chickpeas, cannellini beans, black beans, butter beans

Tinned tuna

Oils – olive oil, neutral-tasting oils, sesame oil

Sugars – caster (superfine), white, icing (confectioners'), brown

Flours – plain (all-purpose), self-raising, cornflour (cornstarch)

Vinegars – balsamic, apple cider, white, white wine

Soy sauce

Spices – large selection including garam masala, coriander and cumin (ground and whole seeds), turmeric powder, nigella seeds, fennel seeds, smoked paprika

Baking powder

Vanilla extract

Fridge

Butter

Yoghurt (full-fat Greek-style and/or plain)

Cheese – feta, cheddar, mozzarella, parmesan

Freezer

Peas

Berries

Corn

Fish fingers

Vegetable scraps

Blackened bananas

Pre-rolled puff pastry sheets

A NOTE ON FOLLOWING THE RECIPES

Between the two of us, we read a lot of cookbooks. It's fun for me, it's work for Simon, but I don't think either of us would do it if we didn't deeply love it. If a recipe jumps out at you, and there's a frisson of chemistry between the recipe on the page, what you've got available, your skills and your sense of 'Yum!' and 'I could do that!', then you should absolutely give it a try. What a great starting point.

In this particular cookbook, we're trying to be there at your side, keeping you on track and chatting about what's going on as you put together your meal. Please read the whole recipe all the way through before attempting it. Do your utmost to follow the recipe faithfully, especially the first time you make it, but also have the common sense to make swaps for things you really don't like. If, for instance, you loathe coriander, you're not suddenly going to like it because it's in Black Bean Tacos (page 43). Use parsley instead, it'll be fine.

Don't forget that what you make might not look like the picture in the book. We have a whole team of food stylists, cooks, home economists and photographers to make our food look bewitching and incredibly attractive.

Taste as you go. Use your powers of observation. Trust what you see, smell and hear, even more than you may trust our recommended cooking times or your timer. Triple-check you're following all the steps in the recipe.

Oh, and before you start cooking ... *wash your fucking hands!*

CUP BOARD

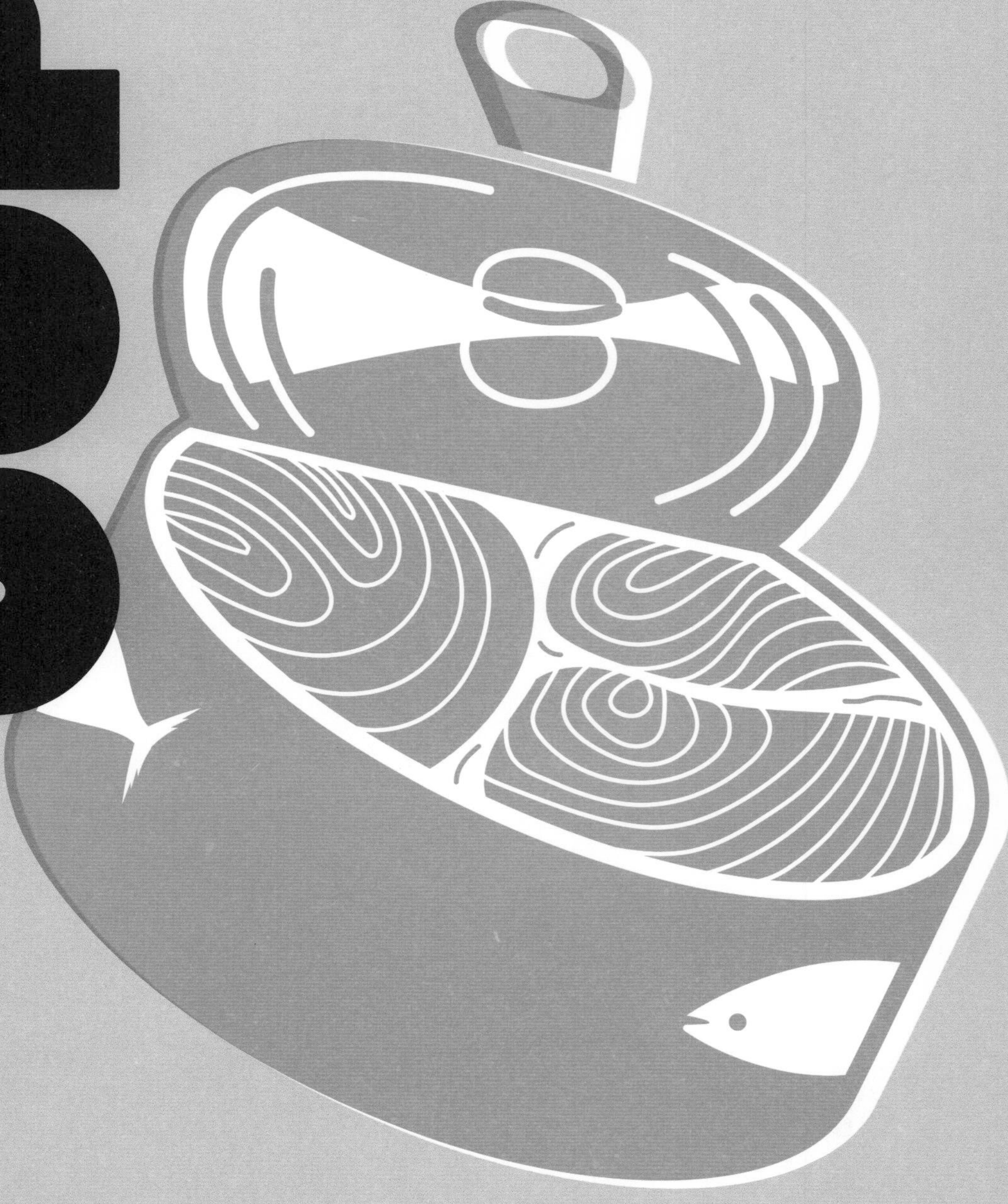

Instant Ramen Noodles, but Good

SERVES 1

2 cups (500 ml) water

120 g (4½ oz) dried ramen

½ cup (30 g) small broccoli florets

1 small handful sugarsnap peas or snow peas (mange tout)

a few pieces of red capsicum (pepper), sliced, or 1 fresh long red chilli, sliced

1 egg

1 spring onion (scallion), greens tops only, finely chopped

I'm an instant-noodle convert thanks to this. — Simon

When I was a kid I'd never had ramen until our family friend Yasuko came to stay. She cooked it for the whole family, we all loved it, it became a staple, and for years after that we only knew it as 'Yasuko-san's Spaghetti'. If someone called it 'ramen' I had no idea what they meant.

The evolution of ramen since then from staple of the impoverished student to something way fancier hasn't stopped me from loving the original super-cheap and easy version. The trick is to not overcook the noodles.

Bring the water to the boil in a small saucepan over medium heat. This will be your soup base, so use more if you want it particularly watery, or less if you prefer it concentrated and salty. (If in doubt, follow the packet directions.)

Add the soup seasoning from the ramen packet, then add the broccoli, sugarsnap or snow peas and capsicum or chilli. Cook for 1 minute, then add the brick of dried noodles. Cook for 1 minute less than the time recommended in the packet directions.

Once the noodles have softened, gently crack the egg into the boiling broth.

As soon as the noodle cooking time is up, use chopsticks or tongs to take the noodles out and put them in your serving bowl.

Watch until the egg looks cooked (it will have lost all translucency, particularly in the bit closest to the yolk, usually after about 3 minutes). Don't stress if it's a bit underdone – the broth will finish the job as you eat. Once the egg is cooked, gently scoop it out and add it to the bowl.

Pour the rest of the broth and vegies into the bowl, top with the spring onion and serve immediately.

1 Don't be devastated if the egg breaks. It happens sometimes.

Emergency Tomato Sauce #1

SERVES 4–6 WITH PASTA

1 onion, peeled and halved crossways

1 garlic clove, peeled

800 g (1 lb 12 oz) tinned chopped tomatoes

2 tablespoons butter

1 handful basil leaves (optional)

salt and pepper

When the fridge is completely bare, or we're on holiday and have just landed in a new kitchen, this is what I make. Based on a classic recipe by Marcella Hazan, it may sound a little odd (butter in a tomato sauce?) and ridiculously simple, but the butter and onion take the edge off the acidity of the tinned tomatoes and leave you with a velvety, sweet and astonishingly tasty sauce. Once you have this recipe up your sleeve, you'll never have to reach for a jar of sauce again.

Pop the onion halves in a saucepan and add the garlic, tomatoes, butter and basil, if using. Bring to a simmer over medium heat, then reduce the heat to low and gently simmer, covered, for 20 minutes, or until the onion is falling apart and the sauce is silky smooth and tastes incredible.

At this point you have a choice – either fish out the sweet, softened onion and garlic clove with a slotted spoon and enjoy the remaining sauce straight or (my preferred option), break up the onion with the wooden spoon and stir it through the tomato to make it a part of the whole (or use a hand-held blender to purée the lot). Either way, season with salt and pepper to taste, then serve with your pasta of choice.

I love this because chopping onions can sometimes be the recipe step that breaks my will to live. — Yumi

1. To make a large batch, just double the quantity of tomatoes and butter and use a large onion.

2. This sauce is extremely adaptable, so I like to play around with the flavourings a bit, depending on what I have to hand. If you have a parmesan rind knocking about, then try adding it at the same time as the onions for extra flavour and fishing it out at the end, or for something a bit more sultry and wintery, add a few pitted black olives and a splash of red wine at the beginning and replace the basil with a few oregano sprigs.

Spaghetti AOP

AOP stands for *aglio, olio e peperoncino* (that's garlic, olive oil and chilli). When you're on your own, you're hungry, it's late at night, you're scrabbling around the cupboards and you just need to get food in fast ... nothing beats this. The sauce cooks in the time it takes to drain the spaghetti and is a full-on blast of heat and flavour. You could shower it with shaved parmesan cheese at the end, stir through some rocket leaves or generally fiddle around with it if you like, but why mess with perfection?

Bring a large saucepan of salted water to the boil. Add the spaghetti and cook for 6–7 minutes, until al dente (taste a strand – if it still has a little bite to it, you're golden).

While the pasta is cooking, very finely chop the garlic and chilli, leaving the chilli seeds in if you like things hot (I do).

Drain the pasta, reserving a little of its cooking water. Return the saucepan to high heat, pour in a thin layer of olive oil, add the garlic and chilli, and fry for 1 minute, until the garlic is just starting to colour.

Add the spaghetti and stir well to coat with the 'sauce', adding a splash of the reserved pasta water if it feels like it needs it.

Season with salt and pepper to taste, tumble it into a bowl, inhale.

1 generous handful (about 125 g/
    4½ oz) dried spaghetti
2 garlic cloves, peeled
1 fresh red chilli
extra virgin olive oil
salt and pepper

1. As with all pasta dishes, don't forget to heavily salt the pasta water before cooking. It makes a huge difference to the flavour and means you add less as seasoning later. Also be sure to cook the pasta in a large enough pan so that it cooks without sticking and clumping together.

2. Please don't try to use quick-cook pasta here – ordinary pasta is quite quick enough as it is. A standard dried spaghetti or (better still) one of those bronze-cut types in the fancy wrapping will do the job perfectly.

3. Of course, the garlic and chilli quantities here depend on your level of tolerance for each. I like lots – as you can see – but if you prefer your dinner less shouty, then do dial it down to a volume that suits you.

Udon Noodles: The Soothing Nood

SERVES 2

Udon noodles are so goddamn easy. The two main things that catch people out are overcrowding and overcooking. Less topping is more. And for that divine slippery, chewy texture, err on the side of undercooking. Once you nail the basics with udon, *then* you can get creative with toppings, adding no more than a couple. Try raw egg yolk, a slice of spiral fish cake (narutomaki), a deep-fried tempura prawn, sliced fried duck breast, bean sprouts, or a simple spoonful of Chilli Crisp Oil (page 205). The spice/condiment shichimi togarashi is good for sprinkling on top.

For years I used powdered, then bottled, soup stock for the broth, but now I make it from scratch – it only takes 5 minutes. But seriously, use the bottled stuff, it's pretty easy to find. I only included the recipe here to show off.

To make the stock, combine all the ingredients in a clean glass jar, give it a little shake, then seal well and refrigerate overnight. The next day, pour the mixture into a small saucepan and bring to the boil over medium heat. Reduce the heat to low and simmer gently for 5 minutes. Strain and store in an airtight container in the fridge until needed. (Thinly slice the strained mushroom and kombu and use them as a condiment in your next bento box or just add them to the soup like we did here.) Note that this is concentrated stock, so don't use it as is.

Prepare the broth by pouring the stock into a medium saucepan. Add an equal amount of water (about 1 cup/250 ml) and placing over medium–low heat. Heat gently and don't be afraid to taste it – it may need a little more water. Leave it to simmer gently while you prepare everything else, taking care not to let it reduce too much.

Meanwhile, in a separate, larger saucepan, boil 3–4 cups (750 ml–1 litre) water. Add the udon noodles and cook according to the packet directions (usually 2–3 minutes), giving them a stir to make sure they don't clump. Drain well and then divide between serving bowls.

While the broth is still simmering, dunk the bok choy into it and count to ten.

Top the noodles with the broth, bok choy, a boiled egg, a garnish of spring onion and a sprinkle of sesame seeds and serve immediately.

MENTSUYU STOCK

100 ml (3½ fl oz) Japanese soy sauce

50 ml (1¾ fl oz) sake (dry rice wine)

50 ml (1¾ fl oz) water

100 ml (3 ½ fl oz) mirin (sweet rice wine)

10 g (¼ oz) dried shiitake mushrooms

10 g (¼ oz) kombu seaweed

UDON NOODLES

1 batch Mentsuyu Stock (above) or 1 cup (250 ml) store-bought udon sauce or kombu tsuyu

400 g (14 oz) ready-to-serve udon noodles

1 bok choy, dirty leaves removed, stem trimmed, halved and washed well

2 soft-boiled eggs, peeled and halved

2 teaspoons finely chopped spring onion (scallion), green tops only

1 teaspoon sesame seeds, toasted

1 Ready-to-serve udon noodles can be found in the Asian food section of supermarkets or in Asian grocers.

2 For great soft-boiled eggs, lower room-temperature eggs into a small saucepan of boiling water and set a timer for 6 minutes. Immediately after the timer sounds, remove the eggs and peel them under cold water.

Crispy Chickpeas

800 g (1 lb 12 oz) tinned chickpeas
2 tablespoons extra virgin olive oil
2 garlic cloves, finely chopped
½ teaspoon smoked paprika
1 teaspoon ground coriander
salt and pepper

MAKES ABOUT 500 G (1 LB 2 OZ)

We're dealing with very *(very)* simple stuff here, but dinner inspiration has to come from somewhere, and sometimes that's as simple as opening the cupboard and giving the first tin you see a little bit of love and attention.

Roasting chickpeas in oil with a little spice until crispy is a great way to transform a pantry staple into something unexpectedly brilliant. Roasting brings out the chickpeas' nuttiness, which combined with their lovely crunchy, toasty golden exterior makes these more than a little moreish. Serve them just as they are with a sprinkle of salt and a few drinks, or give them a starring role in a salad, with some chunks of cucumber, tomato, feta cheese, olives and soft green herbs.

Preheat the oven to 220°C (425°F).

Drain the chickpeas in a colander, rinse well, then pat dry with paper towel or a clean tea towel.

Tip the chickpeas into a large baking dish. Add the olive oil, garlic, paprika and coriander, and season generously with salt and pepper. Give everything a good stir, then roast for 30–40 minutes, or until the chickpeas are lovely and crispy.

Serve warm, sprinkling over a little more salt to taste.

TiPS

1. The spices are my favourites but you can use whatever you prefer.

2. These chickpeas can be made ahead of time and served cold, but if you leave them for a little while they might not remain crispy. In that case you can always toast them in a dry frying pan to bring that crisp back.

3. There are so many ways to use roasted chickpeas in a salad. They are excellent, for example, in a classic tomato salad, with tinned tuna, tossed with grilled Mediterranean vegetables or tucked in among crisp green salad leaves with a yoghurt dressing (page 97).

4. If you're vegan and looking for an egg substitute, the chickpea liquid (or aquafaba) makes a good one. As a rough rule of thumb, 3 tablespoons is equal to one whole egg, and 2 tablespoons is equivalent to one egg white.

Black Pepper No-soak Dal

I was a vegetarian for most of my youth and I honestly thought you could only do one thing with lentils: use the green ones to make a grey, farty lentil soup. It wasn't until I started eating meat again and opting in to vegan and vegetarian food – because I liked it – that I started to understand the hitherto hidden possibilities of this humble legume. A bunch of things make this sexy to me: the low-cost ingredients; the cracking hit of black pepper; the way it can be thrown together on a weeknight in a flash. It also makes brilliant leftovers for work lunches.

Soak the lentils in a bowl of cold water.

For the spice mix, if you're using fresh turmeric, set it aside. Combine the remaining spice mix ingredients, including the turmeric powder, if using, in a small bowl.

Heat the oil in a large, deep frying pan (one that has a lid) over medium heat. Add the peppercorns, cloves and ginger, and the fresh turmeric, if using. Fry for 2 minutes.

Add the tomatoes and fry for at least 10 minutes. (Set a timer to make sure you don't accidentally cheat, because the tomatoes are better cooked until sticky and deep red.) Use your wooden spoon to scrape a little bare hot spot in the frying pan and onto that spot tip the spice mix. Stir to release the aromas, then gradually incorporate the spices into the tomato mixture.

Drain the lentils and add them to the pan, along with the water or stock. Mix well, then put a lid on the frying pan and cook, stirring occasionally, for 25 minutes.

Serve with a fat blob of Greek-style yoghurt and have it on the table so people can add more as they like.

300 g (10½) split red lentils

2 tablespoons neutral-tasting oil (e.g. grapeseed, canola, sunflower)

1 tablespoon peppercorns, crushed

3 cloves

1 tablespoon fresh grated ginger

500–700 g (1 lb 2 oz–1 lb 9 oz) chopped fresh or tinned diced tomatoes

4 cups (1 litre) stock or water

Greek-style yoghurt, to serve (optional but not really)

SPICE MIX

1 teaspoon grated fresh turmeric or turmeric powder

1 teaspoon chilli powder (optional)

1 teaspoon ground coriander

1½ teaspoons salt

1. It's crucial to use medium heat. Don't go blasting the hell out of this dish or you'll burn it on the bottom of the pan and it won't taste any good. Keep an eye on the heat and remember, nuclear isn't necessarily better.

2. The pepper adds a real kick! To lessen its intensity, don't crush the peppercorns, or leave them out completely.

3. If you plan to put this recipe in regular rotation, it's a good idea to measure out batches of the spice combo into separate small containers so that you have a ready-made mix on standby.

Chickpea and Spinach Curry

SERVES 4

about 600 g (1 lb 5 oz) tomatoes or 800 g (1 lb 12 oz) tinned crushed tomatoes

2 teaspoons garam masala

2 teaspoons curry powder

1 teaspoon ground cumin

½ teaspoon pepper

1 teaspoon salt

2 tablespoons coconut oil

800 g (1 lb 12 oz) tinned chickpeas, drained and rinsed

400 ml (14 fl oz) tinned coconut milk

1 tablespoon vegetable stock powder or 800 ml (28 fl oz) vegetable or chicken stock

120 g (4¼ oz) baby spinach, to serve

coriander (cilantro) leaves, to serve (optional)

fresh red banana chilli, sliced, to serve

lime juice, to serve

Every school and uni holidays I've made a point of teaching my teenager a couple of excellent but easy recipes. She's what fitness people call 'coachable' – she listens to and applies advice, which is very satisfying! Seeing my (now adult) kid expanding her repertoire of healthy meals fills me with confidence about her future ability to take care of herself.

She nailed this one immediately, and always sticks to the timers and measures out the spices. Since learning it four months ago, she's successfully replicated it at least seven times. It's been implanted!

Chop the tomatoes, if using fresh. (This is one of those cases where I want you to just chop the fucking tomatoes. Don't overthink it! They don't need to be perfect, just chop 'em rough as – whatever you do will work.) Measure the spices into a small bowl.

Heat the oil in a large saucepan over medium heat, then fry the spices for 2 minutes, stirring them through the oil to release and awaken the aromas. Add the tomatoes and cook for 10–12 minutes, stirring regularly. This is an important step that people sometimes rush, so I recommend setting a timer to give the tomatoes the cook-down they need – they should turn jammy and sweet and incredible.

Add the chickpeas, stir them through for 2–3 minutes, then add the coconut milk. Add the vegetable stock powder and, using the coconut milk tin as a measure, two tins of water. Or add the liquid vegetable stock. Cook for 15 minutes.

To serve, divide the spinach between serving bowls then ladle the curry over the top, garnishing with coriander, if using, chilli slices and a generous squeeze of lime juice.

1. Measuring the spices first saves a lot of stress. In fact, I think this is the best advice I can give you for any dish. You don't want to be already cooking when you're struggling to find that little bag of spices you know you have ... somewhere.

2. Use fresh tomatoes when in season, and tinned ones if not.

3. In cold weather, warm the bowls right before serving by pouring a cup of boiling water into each, leaving for 1 minute, then tipping out.

4. The curry powder you use will have a huge influence on the flavour of the finished dish. The kid I taught this to has a soft spot for Keen's Curry Powder, so when she makes this for me, it tastes a lot like my childhood.

5. *Don't scrimp* on the lime juice. It's essential.

Coconutty Lentil Stew

1 large sweet potato, cut into 1 cm
(½ inch) cubes

2 tablespoons cumin seeds

vegetable oil (or another neutral-
tasting oil, e.g. grapeseed,
sunflower)

salt and pepper

1 onion, thinly sliced

2 garlic cloves, finely grated

1 thumb-sized piece (about
5 cm/2 inches) fresh ginger,
finely grated

1 fresh green chilli, finely chopped
(optional)

1 teaspoon turmeric powder

1 teaspoon ground coriander

1 teaspoon garam masala

500 g (1 lb 2 oz) dried red lentils

400 g (14 oz) tinned coconut cream

2 cups (500 ml) boiling water,
plus extra as needed

1 vegetable stock (bouillon) cube

2⅔ cups (120 g) baby spinach

juice of 1 lemon

Greek-style yoghurt, to serve

toasted flatbreads, to serve

SERVES 6–8

Okay, hands up, I've only called this a stew so I could sneak a second red lentil dal recipe into this book, but this one's really, REALLY good! I love the green in here (to be honest, I'm a big fan of stirring baby spinach into all sorts of dishes like this – not only does it taste great, but it gives me immense pleasure to know I've chucked a ton of extra Popeye-pleasing nutrition in there, too). Yes, you could serve it without the crispy sweet potatoes on top if you're not a fan, but for me they make it.

Preheat the oven to 180°C (350°F).

Arrange the sweet potato pieces on a baking tray in a single layer. Scatter half the cumin seeds over, drizzle a little oil over, season with salt and pepper and roast for 20–25 minutes until golden. Set aside.

Heat a thin layer of oil in a heavy-bottomed saucepan over medium–high heat. Add the onion and the remaining cumin seeds and cook, stirring occasionally, for 8–10 minutes, until the onion is a deep golden brown. Add the garlic and ginger, and cook for another 1 minute, then add the remaining spices and cook for a further 1 minute, stirring constantly, until your whole kitchen smells amazing.

Add the lentils and cook for 1 minute, stirring well to coat them in all that lovely goodness, then pour in the coconut cream and boiling water. Crumble in the stock cube and bring to the boil, then reduce the heat to low and simmer for 25–30 minutes, stirring occasionally and topping up with a few extra splashes of water as needed, until the lentils are soft and the 'stew' has the consistency of a thick, creamy soup. Stir in the baby spinach and cook for a further 1 minute until wilted, then remove from the heat, squeeze in the lemon juice and stir to combine. Season with salt and pepper to taste.

Ladle into bowls, top with the sweet potato pieces and a dollop of Greek-style yoghurt and serve with toasted flatbreads for dipping.

1. Don't be tempted to speed up the onion-cooking stage and go for a lighter shade; this is the all-important base flavour in this dish (and in a lot of other Indian dishes too). You need a deep, bronzed tan that's only just off starting to burn.

2. Coconut cream makes this dish particularly delicious, but if you'd rather keep things lighter you can always use coconut milk (full-fat or reduced-fat) instead.

This scores high on my fart-o-meter. If you don't want high 'gas bills', try swapping onion for fennel like I do on page 38. – Yumi

Rice Done Right: Absorption Method

My mum gave me a rice cooker when I first moved from my home city of Melbourne but I ended up getting rid of it when Sydney's famous cockroaches made a home inside its electrical components. Since then I've been satisfied with making rice in a good saucepan with a tight-fitting lid.

If you're also happy without a rice cooker, then you need to master the cooking of rice. Absorption-method rice has been a staple my whole life, and not a week has gone by when I haven't made at least two batches.

It's not the same as pilaf rice, which has separate grains, and it's not the same as risotto rice, which still has bite. If done correctly, absorption-method rice should stick together without being gluey. It should be soft all the way through and glossy – an individual and a team player. You'll be able to shape it into Onigiri (page 35), use it in hand rolls (page 37), and enjoy it with Yoshiko's Tsukemono (page 215).

Measure out your rice using the same cup or scoop each time. (I leave mine inside the rice container so it's always there.) Pour the rice into the saucepan and add cold water to wash it, stirring your hand through it then draining the water off. (This water is famously good for plants so tip it into a watering can or directly into your plants if you can.) Repeat this rinsing step twice more (three times in total) and then fill the pot up so the water sits from the tip of your finger to the first knuckle above the rice (called the 'first knuckle measure'). It's roughly 1 cm (½ inch). If these esoteric measurements are maddening and you like to do things precisely, you can always use your kitchen scales to weigh the pot, the rice and the water and keep records until you hit the perfect ratio.

Put the lid on the saucepan and leave the rice to soak for at least 15 minutes or at most overnight (if you're planning on cooking it in the morning).

Place the saucepan over high heat with the lid on until the water starts to bubble and get close to overflowing. Immediately reduce the heat to low, then continue to cook until all the water has evaporated (lift the lid briefly to check). For white rice, this whole process should take 12–14 minutes (I recommend setting a timer to figure it out).

Only remove the lid completely when you're ready to serve the rice, and then, remembering that heat is a finite resource, leave the lid on to retain the heat if you're going to want second helpings.

TIPS

1. It's impossible to make good rice if your saucepan is crap, so if you've been trying for years and still haven't nailed good rice, it's probably not your fault. Think about getting an 'investment' saucepan. (I still have my pepper grinder and a saucepan from that year I moved to Sydney.)

2. Sometimes old rice has to be thrown out. This does not make you a failure. Add it to the compost.

Storage and Leftovers

Left-over rice can be a culprit of food poisoning if not stored correctly. To refrigerate rice, transfer it to your best-sized airtight container or a reusable snaplock bag. As soon as the steam stops rising, seal well and put it in the fridge. To minimise the impact of hot rice on the temperature inside your fridge, put frozen ice bricks on top of the containers while they cool. Refrigeration doesn't kill the bacteria, just slows them down, so keep the rice for no longer than 5 days.

Once rice has been refrigerated it completely changes character. It becomes dry and a little charmless. To revive it, decant it into a microwave-safe bowl, sprinkle a teaspoon of cold water over it, cover with a plate and microwave gently for 1½ minutes. (It can be overcooked so aim for low and slow.) In its cold, fridgey state, it can regain excellence by becoming Fried Rice (page 35). But if you know you're not likely to use it for a while, wrap it up in suitable portions and stick it in the freezer (as quickly as outlined above) until needed. You can defrost it in the fridge overnight. It will defrost on your way to work if you're using it for an office lunch. Or defrost it in the microwave using the method above.

LEFT-OVER RiCE

My friend's nonna swears left-over cooked rice is an essential ingredient in her famous pork meatballs; the rice holds its shape and lightens those sweaty, meaty spheres. My mum portions and wraps her left-over rice into single serves and freezes them, pulling out one serve at a time as needed. This suits her little-old-lady lifestyle, where often dinner is a bowl of rice and an assortment of pickles.

For me? I almost ALWAYS have some left-over rice, and usually lots. I try to cook enough rice for generous serves with dinner, plus enough left over that I can make onigiri for the kids' school lunches the next morning.

MAKE THiS

Onigiri

These Japanese rice balls are usually eaten wrapped in nori seaweed, and the ones you buy often have something delicious stuffed in the middle – more seaweed, salmon or pickle. (Not much – a teaspoon-sized portion.) Don't feel pressured though, my entire childhood we ate onigiri with no filling! They were plain balls of rice with a little salt sprinkled on the outside, wrapped in nori.

If the rice is cooked properly (see page 32), it should stick together without needing a binding agent. I find the rice forms a ball and holds its shape better when warm, so when I'm making school-lunch onigiri, I very gently reheat the rice in the microwave. One kid likes her onigiri with avocado and kewpie mayo inside; the other adores it with tuna and kewpie mayo. Either way, I know that they don't have a lot of connection with their Japanese heritage but they freakin' LOVE onigiri.

To make an onigiri with something inside, form a hollow half-snowball of rice in the palm of your (clean, cold, slightly wet) hand. Squeeze about a teaspoon of mayo into the hollow, then tuck in the filling and close up by completing the snowball shape with more rice. Compact the ball tightly with your hands without crushing it. A sprinkle of salt over the top is great. Just before serving, wrap two pieces of seaweed around the outside.

AND THiS

Stir-fried rice

Be sure to start with fridge-cold left-over rice (this is non-negotiable). The rest is more guiding principles than actual recipe – be sure to consider colour when choosing veg, cook everything quick and hot, stirring constantly, and don't overcrowd the pan as you go. DON'T add a new element to the pan until the old one is cooked and hot, and you'll be golden.

Japanese Hand Roll Sushi

SERVES 4 SMALL KIDS OR 2 BIG ONES

Kids love this, it's healthy and it tastes great. I get asked if you need to season the rice with vinegar and sugar as you might have seen done in a sushi shop. I never do.

I've talked on our podcast about 'idiot tax' – the extra money we spend on an unfamiliar ingredient when we don't know the going rate. Japanese ingredients are almost always cheaper, and often better quality, in Asian or specialty Japanese grocery stores than in supermarkets.

You don't need all the fillings. Tuna and avocado can go together. Fish fingers and avocado can go together. Tuna and fish fingers *cannot* go together. And all three can be used on their own.

If you're opening a new packet of seaweed, you won't need to do this, but if your seaweed is still okay but a little flaccid, which can happen when it has been exposed to humidity, revive it by flapping one side lightly over the open flame of your gas stove or over the element of your electric stove for a minute or two.

If using fish fingers, cook them according to the packet directions.

Set out your condiments on the table: soy sauce and a cute side dish of tsukemono (Japanese pickles).

Make sure your benchtop is very dry and clean, then lay out a sheet of seaweed, rough side up. Spread a layer of rice about 8 mm (⅜ inch) thick on top of the seaweed, leaving a 1–2 cm (½–¾ inch) margin at the top and bottom but going all the way to the sides. Make a horizontal line of mayonnaise along the rice, then nestle a row of avocado slices, drained tinned tuna, or two fish fingers alongside.

Roll up the seaweed from bottom to top, tucking in the filling so it sits in the centre of the roll. Turn the roll all the way over so that the seam sits at the bottom. (This helps to seal it.)

Cut the roll in half using a sharp, clean knife, then serve immediately. To eat, dip the roll lightly in soy sauce but please don't drown it. It makes me wince to see people do that.

4 nori seaweed sheets

best-quality soy sauce, to serve

Yoshiko's Tsukemono (page 215), to serve

2½ cups (465 g) freshly cooked or reheated rice (page 32)

Japanese mayonnaise

FILLING

8 fish fingers

1 perfect avocado

370 g tinned tuna

1. The pickles are there as a mouth refresher. They don't need to be shoved into or onto the roll. They can be eaten separately.

2. Enhance the experience with a strong, small cup of genmai-cha, Nihon-cha or a Japanese non-alcoholic beer.

3. If you don't use nori frequently, and/ or you live in a warm climate, be aware that it can lose its snap and become chewy and rancid. It's still edible and won't hurt you – I have even had it served to me like this in Australian restaurants. The best thing you can do to avoid it going bad is store it in a snaplock bag *in the freezer.* It will last for ages in there and defrost in seconds.

Freakin' Fancy Pilaf

SERVES 6

1¾ cups (350 g) basmati rice

⅓ cup (75 g) split moong dal

1 teaspoon cumin seeds

1 teaspoon mustard seeds (optional)

2 sprigs of curry leaves, leaves picked

2 cinnamon sticks

2 tablespoons neutral-tasting oil
(e.g. grapeseed, canola, sunflower)

1 fennel bulb, finely chopped

500 g (1 lb 2 oz) broccoli, head
chopped into florets, stem into
large dice, in separate bowls

¼ cup (60 ml) mirin (sweet rice wine)
or 1½ teaspoons sugar

1 teaspoon salt

⅔ cup (105 g) cashews

2 fresh long green chillies,
finely chopped

500 g (1 lb 2 oz) mixed tomatoes,
small and large, chopped

400 ml (14 fl oz) coconut milk

pinch of saffron, soaking in
200 ml (7 fl oz) water

70 g (2½ oz) pitted dates, chopped

Greek-style yoghurt, to serve

Cultures all over the world have versions of pilaf – or pilau, pelau, pulao, palaw, etc. All cook rice in stock and incorporate other ingredients such as vegetables and nuts. I've been having a whirlwind romance with pilaf because it's a terrific way to use up vegetables, feed a crowd, make a big gluten-free and dairy-free dish, and supply my work week with ample leftovers. Start your own pilaf romance with this recipe, then add your own signature by gradually substituting your preferred vegetables and spices. Serve it as part of a feast, or alongside chicken cutlets, a chickpea curry or even Tofu-skin Pork Rolls (page 114), but it's great on its own.

Rinse the rice and moong dal together in a sieve, then leave them to soak in cold water.

Combine the spices, including the curry leaves, in a small bowl.

Place a large frying pan or low-sided flameproof casserole dish that has a tight-fitting lid (I use a heavy 30 cm/12 inch cast-iron pot) over medium heat. Add the oil and heat until it starts to shimmer, then pour in the spices and stir for 1 minute, using the lid as a shield to minimise the number of mustard seeds popping out of the pan.

Add the fennel, broccoli stem pieces, mirin and salt, and cook, stirring frequently, for at least 10 minutes until caramelised (set a timer to ensure you give it the time it needs). Add the cashews and chilli, stir well, then add the tomatoes. Reduce the heat slightly and cook, stirring frequently, for another 10 minutes.

Drain the rice and moong dal, then add to the pan along with the coconut milk and the saffron and its soaking water. Increase the heat to high and stir the broccoli florets and the dates through. Once the mixture starts to boil again, put the lid on, reduce the heat to low and cook for 25 minutes. Remove from the heat and allow it to rest without removing the lid (not even just for a quick peek) for at least 10 minutes.

Serve direct from the pan with giant dollops of Greek-style yoghurt.

1. You can replace the fennel with onion, in which case you won't need the mirin or sugar.

2. If you happen to be missing a spice, don't worry; it will still be delicious.

3. In case it's not obvious from the ingredients list, this makes a BIG amount of food. Make sure your pan and your tummy can handle it.

Ultimate Quesadillas

SERVES 1 (MULTIPLY AS NECESSARY)

These quesadillas are pretty much the ultimate five-minute food fix. From cupboard to table in the time it takes to listen to your favourite podcast *coughs*, they fit the bill for those days when only a meal with zero prep time and 5 minutes' cooking will do. (And reader, we have a lot of those days.)

You can use any type of cheese, although as this tends to be an emergency meal, I often use grated tasty or cheddar straight from the bag as option 1. If you want to get fancy, a smoked cheddar works really well for flavour, while a grated mozzarella or pizza cheese will provide that nice stretchy pull. The bacon jam brings a little something extra to all the cheesy, carby goodness. Leave it out or replace it with a little of your favourite tangy relish or sauce if you'd prefer.

Heat a frying pan or a barbecue chargrill plate to medium–hot.

Brush the pan or barbecue chargrill plate with olive oil, then throw on one of the tortillas and press it down. Dollop a tablespoon of the bacon jam into the centre of the tortilla, spread it out to the edges using the back of the spoon, then scatter the grated cheeses over. Top with the second tortilla and press it down to squash it into its friend.

Brush the surface of the tortilla sandwich with oil and cook for 2 minutes, then flip and cook the other side for a further 2 minutes, or until golden on both sides with molten cheese in the middle. The tortilla changes character when cooked, becoming flaky and golden and releasing a toasty aroma.

Remove from the pan, cut into quarters and serve hot.

olive oil

2 mini tortillas or flatbreads

1 tablespoon Bacon Jam (page 209; optional)

1 tablespoon grated cheese number 1

1 tablespoon grated cheese number 2

I consider bacon jam to be an act of digestive violence and won't touch the stuff. I *will*, however, switch it for ham. – Yumi

TIPS

1   These are great for camping or as a side to something more substantial, such as a chilli stew or the filling for the Black Bean Tacos on page 43, but they make a perfectly acceptable main gig too.

2   To provide a little light relief from all that cheese (and to up the dairy content of this excellent meal yet further), try dipping these in a bowl of Greek-style yoghurt with 1 teaspoon smoked paprika swirled through. Cold yoghurty dip and hot, toasted cheesy bread = killer combo.

Black Bean Tacos

SERVES 2 (3 TACOS PER PERSON)

I love tacos, but the pressure to prepare toppings, sauces and fancy accoutrements puts me off. So what are the essentials of a good taco that we can keep? And what fussy bits can we ditch? Lime, coriander and avocado are my favourite elements. I've always loved a good bottled hot sauce, and sour cream is a must, plus the taco itself, of course. As a kid I used to love those giant crunchy tacos, mostly because they're as processed and junk-foody as a corn chip. Nowadays I'm a fan of the simple flour tortilla, which when gently toasted becomes a giant in the gorgeousness of its aromas and textures.

Cut the avocado into slim wedges and lightly sprinkle with the extra salt.

Heat the oil in a large non-stick frying pan over medium heat. Add the garlic, salt, paprika and cumin, and fry for 2 minutes, taking care not to scorch the ingredients. Add the black beans, then stir well to coat in the oil and spice mixture. (This is an important step because it transforms ordinary tinned beans into something rather wonderful.) Fry for 3 minutes then add the apple cider vinegar and stir well, crushing the beans a little with the back of the spoon.

When ready to serve, warm the tortillas your favourite way – in a dry frying pan, perhaps, or the microwave. My favourite way to serve them is to fold them gently in half and pop them in the toaster. They need roughly the same amount of time as a lightly cooked piece of toast and they should come out slightly puffed, fluffy on the inside, semi-crisp on the outside and smelling amazing.

Assemble each taco by starting with a good 2 tablespoons of sour cream in the warmed taco shell. It will slip and slide around as it melts, but this is the idea. Quickly top with a modest scoop of black bean mixture and moisten the beans with a generous shake of hot sauce. Add a few slices of avocado, a generous garnish of coriander, a sprinkle of red chilli, a crumble of feta and then, finally, a squeeze of lime juice. Eat immediately.

1 ripe but firm avocado

1 tablespoon grapeseed or vegetable oil

1 garlic clove or 2 teaspoons garlic-infused olive oil

½ teaspoon salt, plus extra for sprinkling

½ teaspoon smoked paprika

½ teaspoon ground cumin

400 g (14 oz) tinned black beans, drained and rinsed

2 tablespoons apple cider vinegar

6 small flour tortillas (about 14 cm/5½ inches in diameter)

⅔ cup (160 g) sour cream

hot sauce, to serve

½ bunch coriander (cilantro), leaves picked

1 fresh long red chilli, thinly sliced

100 g (3½ oz) feta cheese

1 lime, cut into wedges

TIPS

1. If you don't want the chilli too hot, remove the seeds before chopping.

2. I sometimes put the toaster on the table so we can each toast our own tortillas. I love them fresh and hot.

3. Doubling the bean mixture is a good idea so that you have extra if you get a bad case of the second-helpings, or you can make a beans and cheese toastie another day. Store leftovers in an airtight container in the fridge for up to 3 days.

Flatbread Pizzas Four Ways

160 ml (5¼ fl oz) tomato passata
(puréed tomatoes)

4 store-bought pitta breads

100 g (3½ oz) pizza cheese

TOPPINGS

8 pitted kalamata olives,
drained and quartered

2 slices ham, roughly torn into
1 cm (½ inch) pieces

8 cherry tomatoes, halved

50 g (1¾ oz) feta cheese

1 small zucchini (courgette),
sliced into ribbons using
a vegetable peeler

extra virgin olive oil or
Chilli Crisp Oil (page 205)

1 small handful basil leaves,
roughly torn

SERVES 4

I'm very proud of these little pizzas. There's something seriously magical about ripping open a packet of flatbreads; throwing on some passata, grated cheese and a few things from the fridge; and moments later having a meal on the table the whole family will ask for time and time again.

The devil here is in the details. Firstly, only a ripping-hot oven will do. Secondly, for a tasty, crisp base, put your pizzas on something blistering hot from the get-go. You can use a pizza tray, but my favourite is an inverted baking tray. Have one fired up on each shelf and you've mastered the art of the pantry pizzaiola.

Preheat the oven to 250°C (500°F) or its highest setting. Arrange four oven trays or pizza trays in the oven on different shelves.

Place 2 tablespoons of the passata in the middle of one of the flatbread bases then, using the back of the spoon, work it out towards the edges so that it covers the base leaving a thin margin around the outside. Repeat with the remaining bases and passata, then sprinkle over the cheese to cover evenly.

Scatter half the olive quarters over one pizza base and set aside. Scatter the ham over another. Dot the cherry tomatoes over a third pizza base and roughly crumble over the feta, then scatter the zucchini and remaining olives on the final base. Drizzle a little extra virgin olive oil or chilli crisp oil over each pizza, then transfer to the hot trays in the oven and cook for 3–4 minutes until the pizzas are golden and crisp around the edges and the cheese is molten and bubbling (if the bases are really nice and hot you'll even get a little bubbling in the bread just like a real pizza). Remove from the oven, scatter the basil leaves over the cherry tomato and zucchini pizzas, cut into slices and serve immediately.

TIPS

1. The choice of flatbreads is important – I like to use the large pitta flatbreads from my local supermarket but, as with making your own dough, you might need to do a little experimenting until you find your perfect base.

2. If you really can't stand the idea of not making your own dough, Yumi's Two-ingredient Bread (page 47) works well. Just be sure to roll it out nice and thin and give it an extra few minutes in the oven.

3. You can, of course, top your pizzas however you like – just don't overload them with toppings. Less is always more, especially when it comes to the cheese.

Two-ingredient Bread

SERVES 3–6

One of the things that can bring inexperienced cooks undone is mess. And I don't know if this is good news or bad, but the more you cook, the more you develop shit-hot cleaning skills. It's not just about becoming more efficient at cleaning; it's about not getting grouchy about having to clean in the first place. Cleaning is just part of the glorious slosh that goes into eating well. Making any kind of bread involves making a bit of a mess, but after a few goes you'll know how to minimise it and clean it up painlessly.

This bread is a doozy. It requires just two ingredients, plus some very therapeutic (and quick) kneading, and it levels up *any* meal. Serve it alongside any of the curries in this book, the Chicken and Sweet Potato Soup on page 103, or to mop up the delicious juice left behind from Simon's Asparagus and Parmesan Salad (page 80).

Mix the flour, yoghurt and salt, if using, together in a bowl. Once it comes together, tumble it out onto the benchtop and knead with clean, dry hands for 3–4 minutes. As you knead, try to pick up any stray, shaggy bits of dough left behind on the benchtop and the bowl so that by the end of the 3 minutes the benchtop looks almost clean. (If your dough is sticking and your benchtop is a mess, your mixture is too wet – just add a couple of handfuls of flour as you knead. If it won't come together, wet your hands and keep kneading.) Once the dough is smooth and forms a neat ball, pop it back into the bowl, cover and leave it for at least 10 minutes to rest. (You can leave it for several hours until you're ready to eat.)

Cut the dough into six even pieces, each weighing about 45 g (1½ oz). Sprinkle each ball with a little more flour, then roll them out on a clean benchtop to about 16 cm (6¼ inches) in diameter (or you can leave them thicker if you prefer). Coat one side with sesame seeds, if you like.

Heat a dry frying pan over high heat and cook the flatbreads one at a time for 2–3 minutes each side. Alternatively, for a different effect, try spraying the frying pan lightly with oil spray for the first side, then spraying the bread itself before flipping it over to cook the second side. Keep them warm by covering with foil or popping them in a 100°C (200°F) oven.

Serve hot.

1 cup (150 g) self-raising flour, plus extra for dusting

½ cup (130 g) plain or Greek-style yoghurt

pinch of salt (optional)

sesame seeds (optional)

cooking oil spray (optional)

1. If you don't have a rolling pin, the side of a large, clean, food-safe spray can will do the job. I used cans of canola oil spray for years (and was quite proud of myself). Eventually I found a rolling pin I liked for $4 in Chinatown, and I did notice it was quite a lot easier to grip!

2. This recipe works with gluten-free self-raising flour, but the flatbreads won't roll out as big. Roll each 45 g (1½ oz) ball into a 14 cm (5½ inch) flatbread, or instead of making six flatbreads out of the mixture, make four bigger balls about 65 g (2¼ inches) each.

3. This recipe works with lactose-free yoghurt – there's no discernible difference.

LOVING YOUR LOAF

'Man cannot live on bread alone' went one of the hymns I sang at school as a kid. While I can't recall the rest, this bit struck me as completely wrong. If nutrition wasn't a thing, I could quite happily live on bread alone – I love the stuff more than it's healthy to admit, and our house is never without at least a loaf or two on the go at any one time. In my years of eating bread in all its shapes and forms I've compiled a few thoughts on the matter, which I hope will take your appreciation of the humble loaf to new heights.

CHOOSING

Pick the right bread for the right moment. This is very simple but very important. I'm a firm believer that *all* bread is good and that we should think of it as an essential, after which it comes down to choosing the right bread for the right circumstances. There's a time and place for pretty much everything. You wouldn't wear a ballgown to the beach or a singlet to the office. Don't make the same mistake with your loaf.

A freshly baked baguette, for example, is the perfect choice for a brie and tomato sandwich – the soft, delicate interior absorbs the fruit's juices while that crisp, crackling carapace delivers up the essential contrast. A dark rye bread, with its dense texture and treacly flavours, provides the perfect foil for the strong tastes of cured fish and meats. And while I love an artisan sourdough every bit as much as the next person, it will never be the right choice for a ham and cheese toastie. Be guided by these twin principles of texture and flavour, and you won't go too far wrong.

TOASTING

Toast is *always* a good idea and should certainly not be restricted to the breakfast table. There's no perfect way to toast, of course, but it's worth pushing the toasting that bit further than you think is a good idea – after all, it's called toast and not hot bread for a reason. While you don't want it completely carbonised, the crunch is the whole point. In its purest form, I like mine toasted almost to the point of burnt, slathered in butter and seasoned with a light sprinkling of sea salt flakes, but I'm very happy to top it with pretty much anything I have to hand. What you pick is entirely up to you. Some of my favourites include:

✳ chunky peanut butter and dark chocolate chips

✳ smashed fresh raspberries and honey

✳ hummus and feta

✳ left-over bolognese (page 118)

✳ roughly chopped roasted capsicum (page 87)

✳ camembert and cornichons

✳ mashed overripe banana and ricotta.

STORING

Where you keep your loaf depends, to a certain extent, on where you live. I like to keep mine in a bread bin, but if you live in a very hot or humid climate, you might find it's better to store it in the fridge to prevent it going mouldy too quickly.

If you've bought a loaf of fancy bread and you want to be sure it doesn't go to waste, slice it and store any slices you don't think you'll get through in time in the freezer, ready for toasting. They'll be perfect toasted straight from frozen.

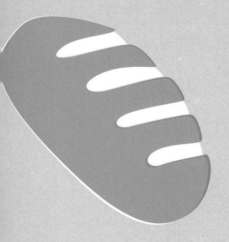

From time to time you might have a bit of left-over bread. It's what you do with it that counts. You can turn it into croutons (page 204), or breadcrumbs, or – my favourite – do as the Italians do and toast it, rub it with garlic and shove it in the bottom of a bowl of soup.

Roast Potatoes Two Ways

Crispy, crunchy and inescapably moreish, the roast potato may just be one of my favourite things to eat. But only if done right.

These recipes give you two very different roast potato options – one following the traditional English/Irish method (with a little cheat for achieving that crunchy exterior), the other taking its cue from the Italian way of prepping the humble spud. For weekends when roast meats are ticking away in the oven, the go-slow route is the one to take, but for midweek meals (and particularly as an accompaniment to grilled meats or fish) it's the Italian job all the way – 20 minutes from chopping board to plate, with no fiddly peeling. It's as speedy as roasties get.

Slow English

SERVES 6–8

1.5 kg (3 lb 5 oz) potatoes
olive oil
1–2 tablespoons instant polenta
salt, to serve

Peel the spuds, then cut in half and half again.

Lower the potatoes into a large saucepan of lightly boiling water and parboil for 5 minutes over medium heat, then drain and leave to sit in the colander to dry out.

Preheat the oven to 180°C (350°F). Pour a thin layer of olive oil into a large roasting tin, then place it in the oven and heat until smoking.

Tumble the potatoes back into the saucepan, add the instant polenta, cover with a lid and give the pan a vigorous shake so the edges of the potatoes ruffle up.

Remove the tin from the oven and carefully add the potatoes in an even layer (the oil should be so hot the potatoes sizzle). Brush the potatoes all over with the oil, then transfer to the oven and roast for 45 minutes, occasionally removing the tray from the oven and turning the potatoes, until lightly golden.

Remove the roasting tin from the oven, crank the temperature up to 220°C (425°F), drain the excess oil from the tin, then return the potatoes to the oven for 10–20 minutes, until deep brown and crispy all over.

Serve with plenty of salt.

 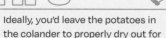

TiPS

1. Ideally, you'd leave the potatoes in the colander to properly dry out for at least 30 minutes before you start roasting. If you haven't planned that far ahead, just add them to the pan after draining and carry on as before, but don't expect them to be quite so crispy and delicious.

2. You don't need the polenta here, but if you like your potatoes really crispy and crunchy, this will push them even further in that direction.

HOLD YOUR NERVE and cook these for the full 1 hour, 20 mins. Freakin' amazing. – Yumi

Quick Italian

SERVES 2–4

Preheat the oven to 220°C (425°F).

Cut the unpeeled potatoes in half, then cut each half into roughly 2 cm (¾ inch) pieces – about the size of your thumb tip. Strip the rosemary needles from the stalks and chop finely. Using the flat of a knife or the palm of your hand, squash the garlic cloves so they break up but are still in their skins.

Pour a thin layer of olive oil into a large roasting tin, then place it in the oven and heat until smoking.

Remove the tin from the oven and carefully add the potatoes in an even layer, together with the rosemary and garlic. Brush the potatoes all over with the oil, then transfer to the oven and roast for 20 minutes, occasionally removing the tray from the oven and turning the potatoes, until golden all over.

Serve with plenty of salt.

1 kg (2 lb 4 oz) potatoes
2 rosemary sprigs
4–6 garlic cloves
olive oil
salt, to serve

1   You may need to use a spatula to turn the potatoes and to remove them from the tin to serve, as some might stick to the tin. That's perfectly okay (good even) – just scrape up the delicious little crispy bits and serve with the rest.

2   These potatoes are, to my mind, particularly fantastic because you really don't have to peel them. Result! If, however, potato peel bothers you, then by all means go ahead and take it off for compost. Just be aware that you've given yourself an extra 5 minutes of hassle and you've lost all the nutrients that reside in it to boot.

Potato Crisp

3 very large potatoes
   (total 450–600 g/1 lb–1 lb 5 oz)

1½ tablespoons olive oil

salt

thyme or rosemary sprigs

SERVES 2–4

I've made this dish hundreds of times, and it's always a hit. As with Simon's potato recipes, the flavour of the spuds takes centre stage, as it should. A version of this appeared in my last cookbook, but I've since made a couple of improvements.

My main criteria when deciding whether or not to make this is whether I have the full 45-minute cooking time available. And it takes a little longer to prep than most of my dishes because of the hand-slicing and the time required to arrange the slices of potato on the baking tray.

Preheat the oven to 200°C (400°F). Boil a kettle-full of water. Clear the sink of dishes. Have some clean rubber gloves and a colander on standby.

Trim the potatoes of any discoloured spots and scrub off any dirt. Using your sharpest knife, cut the potatoes into neat slices about 2 mm (¹⁄₁₆ inch) thick.

Put the potato slices in a large, heatproof bowl in the sink, put on the rubber gloves and, taking care not to scald yourself, pour the boiling water over the potatoes. Slosh them around and separate any slices that are sticking together. Give this process 2 minutes, then tip the whole lot into the colander and drain well, shaking it gently to remove as much water as possible.

While the potatoes are still in the colander, pour over 1 tablespoon of the olive oil and use your hands to mix it through so that all the slices are covered.

Arrange the potatoes on a baking tray (I use a roulade tray) as if you're spreading decks of cards – in rows of overlapping pieces. This can seem like it'll take a long time but a) it doesn't if you move quickly. Don't overthink it (one of my kitchen mottos) and don't aim for perfection (oh, that's another); and b) it's worth the effort of layering because it maximises the edges of potato facing upward and therefore the amount of crispiness.

Cover with a light sprinkle of salt, add the thyme or rosemary sprigs, then drizzle the remaining olive oil over.

Bake for 45 minutes, checking for crispiness after 35 minutes. You may need to rotate the tray 180 degrees halfway through to ensure even cooking. Some ovens may burn the edges of the potato to black. If it looks like it's burning, take it out.

1. Large, choad-like potatoes give the most satisfyingly uniform circles of potato when sliced; I have learned to spot these from 5 metres at the market! You only need three big ones.

2. If you have a large group of people to feed and need to scale this recipe up, use two trays.

Clockwise from top left: Slow English Roast Potatoes (page 50), Potato Crisp, Quick Italian Roast Potatoes (page 51).

Quinoa Burgers

1 cup (200 g) uncooked quinoa

400 g (14 oz) tinned adzuki beans, rinsed and drained

220 g (7¾ oz) medium-firm tofu

⅓ cup (20 g) nutritional yeast

1 tablespoon tomato paste (concentrated purée)

½ teaspoon best-quality salt, plus extra to cook

lots of pepper

grapeseed oil, for frying

SERVES 6

I've always thought burgers would be better without the burger inside. Whether it's a low-rent fast-food chain or a bougie restaurant charging $30, there's something about a meat patty I find unholy and disgusting. (I'm right. Fight me.) Unless, of course, it's vegetarian, in which case I love it, give it to me. A crispy outside, a medley of mysteries within, the intriguing interaction with the sauces and toppings, and how the whole thing hangs together? I especially love a vegie burger that's free of floury binding agents, dried-out bits of corn and dreaded onion. This recipe is surprisingly quick and easy, and married with that chutney you've been saving? Delightfully delicious.

Cook the quinoa according to the packet directions, then transfer to a large bowl and add all the other ingredients except the frying oil. Mix everything together well, mashing the tofu and smashing the adzuki beans as you go – kneading everything, even! – until well combined.

Shape the mixture into six patties, each about 155 g (5½ oz) and about 11 cm (4¼ inches) in diameter. Spread them out on a tray and refrigerate until needed, at least 2 hours.

To cook, preheat a large non-stick frying pan over a medium heat and coat the bottom with a good 1–2 tablespoons grapeseed oil. When the oil is hot, carefully set two or three patties down and fry them for at least 3 minutes, leaving them alone and allowing them to get a good crisp on before attempting to flip them over with a spatula. Sprinkle with a light pinch of salt as they cook. Cook on the other side for about 3 minutes, until crisp. Keep the patties warm on a plate in a 100°C (200°F) oven while you cook the remaining patties.

I love to nestle the quinoa patties in a fresh white bun with relish or chutney, tomato slices, lettuce, two slices of cheese (because one is never enough) and mayo. Add a slice of tinned pineapple and beetroot if desired, and expect to make a mess of your shirt.

For a vegie burger ... this one's ace. – Simon

1 Freeze any spare uncooked burgers as they cook magnificently from frozen.

Excellent Tuna Salad

SERVES 4 GENEROUSLY

Between jobs, studying and travelling I used to return to my mum's cafe to do shifts as a sandwich hand. In the end I reckon I tallied up hundreds of hours and thousands of sandwiches. One of the most popular menu items was the tuna salad, which was incredibly fresh and crunchy and moreish. People used to order it by the container-load. You can shovel quite a lot of it onto a wrap, sandwich or bread roll, or scoop it up with crackers.

Wash and dry all the vegetables. Seed the capsicum and chop it and the celery stalks into 5 mm (¼ inch) dice. Chop the celery leaves. Trim the spring onions, and finely chop. Mix the chopped vegetables, parsley and tuna in a large bowl. Add the mayonnaise and gently mix in, taking care not to overmix – you absolutely *do not* want to turn the tuna into a paste. Allow some of the flakes of tuna to retain their shape and integrity.

Refrigerate immediately in an airtight container and use within 1 week.

1 small red capsicum

3 spring onions (scallions),
    green tops only

150 g (5½ oz) celery stalks and leaves

4 tablespoons finely chopped parsley

425 g (15 oz) tinned tuna,
    well drained

½ cup (120 g) mayonnaise

This would be so good with Greek-style yoghurt instead of mayo! – Simon

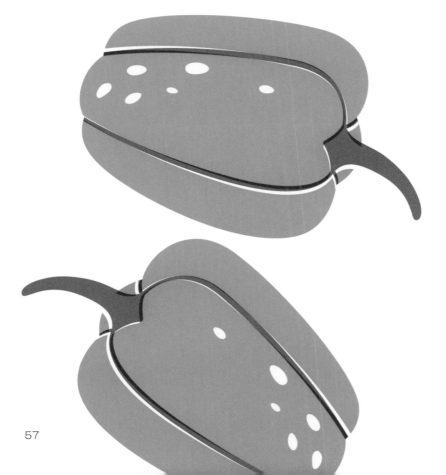

1   This makes a fantastic and nourishing work or school lunch. It's not as fishy-smelling as regular tuna can be and shouldn't upset any grumpy bums working nearby.

2   I've been saving and replanting spring onion bottoms for years now. Cut them off at least 1 cm (½ inch) long, then plant them directly in a pot of soil.

3   I talk about stock on page 103. The spring onion tops, bottoms and parsley stems can all be frozen and used in a future stock.

4   I like to use Norganic brand Golden Soya mayonnaise.

Easy-peasy Overnight Oats

2 cups (190 g) rolled oats

1–2 pears

2 cups (500 ml) water or your milk
of choice, or a mixture of the two,
plus extra milk (optional), to serve

plain or Greek-style yoghurt, to serve

peeled and sliced papaya (optional)

SERVES 4

I must've been in a suggestible phase when I read an ABC article on the four plant-based foods we all need to eat more of: oats, tomatoes, mushrooms, and orange vegetables like pumpkin and sweet potato. It influenced my eating massively! (Clearly I have no regrets and feel magnificent.) For a fantastic way to get more tomatoes inside you, please try Simon's Pan Con Tomate (page 69), which truly is his gift to us all.

But for more oats? As someone often cooking for one, making porridge and the resulting dirty saucepans seems undeniably grim. This soaking method gets me eating oats on the reg without the hassle of scrubbing pots. But also – these are bloody great if you've been a legend and prepped them the night before and then the next morning you need breakfast but you're running late for work. They're perfect for snatching outta the fridge on your way out the door to eat at work or even *ahem* while driving.

Pour the oats into a container that has an airtight lid. Grate the pears onto the oats. Stir the pears through the oats then stir in the water and/or milk. Seal the container and refrigerate overnight.

Spoon servings into a ceramic bowl and either eat as is, or microwave for 1½ minutes. Top with yoghurt and papaya, if using, and if you like, your favourite milk.

1. I'm not an oat snob. The cheaper the better, I say! But do NOT use instant oats. Those are wallpaper glue disguised as food.

2. I used to use all milk, but I honestly couldn't taste the difference when I used water.

3. The pear quantity you use depends on how peary you like your porridge. My optimum is two. I buy half a dozen at a time and ripen them on the windowsill. They can take weeks to really soften and get a flavour up.

A LITTLE NOTE ON NUTRITION

(OR HOW TO EAT TO LIVE FOREVER)

You can drive yourself up the wall trying to make every meal nutritious. And trust me, that's no fun for anyone.

One of the keys to ensuring you get your nutrition in is to actually stop thinking about it over the course of one meal and instead start thinking about it over the course of a day, or even a week. Do this and it suddenly doesn't seem so bad that one meal (*coughs* pasta) is close to 100 per cent carbs, because tomorrow's lunch and dinner are packed with meat and vegies, or salad and fruit.

Obviously, there are whole galaxies of information out there about this, but in short, when it comes to eating for nutrition and wellbeing, you'd be hard pressed to find better advice than that of the great food writer Michael Pollan: 'Eat food, not too much, mostly plants.' It's gold, and is something to live by.

Try and get your fruit and vegies in, go for as many colours as you can, and eat the ones you like so it's not a chore. (And don't be afraid to serve things raw – not only does this save you time, but it's sometimes as good as it's going to be. A perfectly ripe mango, for example, is just that – perfect as it is.)

Also gauge which foods make you feel really good afterwards and steer yourself towards eating more of those. (Yumi loves to eat silken tofu, for example, as she likes how it leaves her feeling full but not heavy, and I could swear I feel better after eating a plate of sushi or a piece of nicely grilled fish.) Just remember, don't eat too much of any one thing and you'll be good. And if you're cooking from scratch, your food won't have processed rubbish in it and will be naturally much better for you. This is already a major win.

Tinned Peaches Delight

SERVES 4–6

This dessert is more than the sum of its pantry-heavy parts and that's surprising, because all those individual parts are pretty incredible.

Tinned peaches are so handy to have in your cupboard – it's like having instant access to perfectly poached fruit whenever you need it. While they're fantastic just as they are (or with a little vanilla ice cream) this takes things up a notch. So much so that I'd happily put this dish on the table when I have friends over and they'd think I'd gone to a lot of effort.

Which, of course, would be a lie.

Toast the nuts in a large frying pan over medium heat for 5–6 minutes, shaking the pan occasionally, until lightly golden. Set aside.

Pour half the cream into a large bowl and beat using a whisk or hand-held electric beaters until soft peaks form. Put the raspberries in a separate bowl and, using the back of a fork, crush them roughly, then fold them through the cream to create a beautiful pink marbled mess.

To make the walnut butterscotch caramel, heat the brown sugar, butter and salt in a small saucepan over low heat until they melt together and start to bubble, then add the remaining cream and whisk until the sauce thickens a little. Add the walnuts, reserving a few for a garnish, and stir to coat the nuts in the sauce.

To serve, arrange two peach halves on a plate. Spoon the sauce over, add a dollop of the raspberry cream and scatter over a few of the reserved toasted walnuts.

120 g (4½ oz) walnut halves

300 ml (10½ fl oz) thick (double) cream

125 g (4½ oz) raspberries

50 g (1¾ oz) soft brown sugar

1 tablespoon butter

pinch of salt

825 g (1 lb 13 oz) tinned peaches

As with all Simon's recipes, this is better if you read it in an English accent. – Yumi

 TIPS

1. If raspberries aren't in season and/or they're looking pricey at the shops, you can leave them out. Instead, try adding 1 teaspoon vanilla extract or rosewater to the cream, to push the dessert in a different (but no less enticing) direction.

2. Don't be scared of making the caramel sauce here. It's a very simple one and, unlike a dry caramel which is easy to burn, not much can go wrong. This might sound odd, but if you fancy experimenting with the flavours of the caramel, try replacing the walnuts with pine nuts and adding ½ teaspoon finely chopped fresh rosemary leaves. Delicious!

INTO

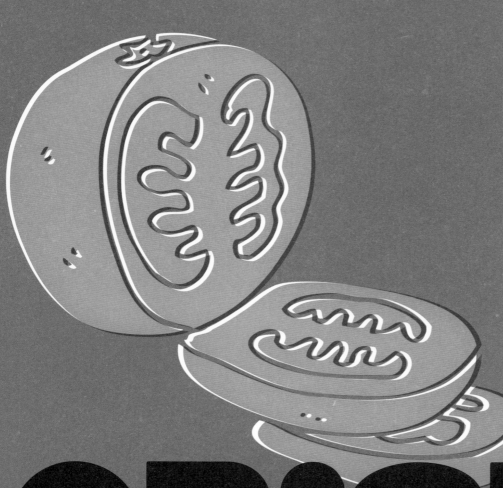

CRISP

Salad Dressing 101

Making salad dressing is about balancing the input of the two star players: oil and whatever you've got that's sour. The sour is often vinegar or lemon juice, and the oil is often olive oil – but it can be macadamia, sesame, walnut, avocado or hemp seed oil, among others. The ratio you're aiming for is roughly 3 parts oil to 1 part vinegar or lemon juice.

Given that there are so few other elements, there's nowhere to hide if one or both of those two ingredients is no good. And here's the good news: Australian-made olive oil will pretty much always be good. The Australian olive oil industry is fantastic – with high standards and reliable quality and supply. Unlike imported oils, locally grown oil won't have been sitting in hot shipping containers for months and should be fresh and young and full of vigour.

Think of oil as something a little like butter. It does last, yes, but it does also turn, and it can be pretty evil if it's rancid. In warmer climates, many of us keep our oils in the fridge to extend shelf life.

Reliable sour elements come in a wide variety of vinegars, which are almost as numerous and varied as wine varieties. Avoid store-bought 'reductions', which are often sugary syrups, and try to avoid knock-off 'balsamic' vinegars, which are often regular vinegar with sugar and colouring added. Sour flavours can also come from lemon juice, lime juice or verjuice.

The other important elements in a salad dressing are salt and sugar. The salt can come from actual salt, or from something like mashed anchovies, dijon mustard or finely chopped capers. The sugar often exists in the vinegar, particularly one of the sweeter vinegars such as balsamic or sherry vinegar. Sweetness can also be added in the form of honey, maple syrup, pomegranate molasses or a reduction of blood orange juice.

Basic Vinaigrette

MAKES ENOUGH FOR 2 FAMILY SALADS

40 ml (1¼ fl oz) white
    balsamic vinegar
⅓ cup (80 ml) olive oil
1 teaspoon honey
1 teaspoon wholegrain mustard
¼ teaspoon salt
½ garlic clove, finely grated (optional)

This is a game-changer and it's really, really delicious. My favourite is to dress a butter lettuce with nothing more than this dressing, then mop up whatever is left on the plate with some good bread. The trick is using the freshest olive oil you have, and a white balsamic vinegar, which is brighter and wears less heavy make-up than regular balsamic.

Combine everything in a jar and shake vigorously.

Celery Salad

700–800 g (1 lb 9 oz–1 lb 12 oz)
  celery

juice of 1 lemon

50 ml (1¾ fl oz) olive oil

1 teaspoon seeded mustard

½ teaspoon salt

½ teaspoon freshly ground
  black pepper

¼ cup (40 g) dried currants

½ cup (80 g) smoked almonds,
  chopped

There are surprisingly few celery salad recipes out there in the wild, which makes no sense given celery is available everywhere, and it's cheapish and actually yummy. After years spent looking for a celery salad recipe I eventually came up with my own, which has so far confounded my efforts to make it more sophisticated. Every time I try adding a new ingredient, it just takes away from what was already excellent. Its simplicity is marvellous – accepting that simplicity is the challenge.

Wash the celery well, then trim off the rough ends but keep the leaves. Dry the stalks using a clean tea towel. Slice the celery into crescents about 3 mm (⅛ inch) thick and put them in a big bowl.

In a small jug, mix the lemon juice, olive oil, mustard, salt and pepper and stir vigorously to emulsify. Add the currants and mix again. Pour the dressing over the celery and you'll immediately see it pick up the shine of the mixture and look lively and tasty. Add the celery leaves and toss well, then scatter the almonds over. Serve immediately.

Crunchy and full of flavour,
this has genuinely made me
see celery in a different light.
The leftovers keep surprisingly
well. – Simon

1. It's worth drying the celery because otherwise water will stick to it and make for a watery salad.

Pan Con Tomate

SERVES 1 (MULTIPLY AS NECESSARY)

Thanks to the globe-conquering phenomenon that is the pizza, we're all extremely familiar with the combination of tomato and bread. But there are plenty of other ways to put these two mighty ingredients together, including this Catalan speciality, which, to my mind, tops the lot.

Grating the tomato seems to really bring out the flavour of even the saddest and hardest of fruit. There must be some science at work here – something about breaking down cell walls to release flavour compounds – that I'm sure someone like Heston Blumenthal would get very excited about. All I know is that something this simple shouldn't be this delicious. It feels like cheating.

Toast or grill the bread to your liking (I like mine lightly charred) and place on a plate.

Coarsely grate the tomatoes into a large bowl, saving the left-over tomato skins to make stock (see page 103). Finely grate the garlic clove into the bowl, then drizzle the olive oil over and mix everything together well. Season with salt and pepper.

To serve, generously spread the tomato purée over the toast. Add a little extra drizzle of oil and sprinkle a little extra salt over to finish.

2 slices bread

2 tomatoes

½ small garlic clove

2 tablespoons extra virgin olive oil, plus extra to serve

salt and pepper

You can take this over to a friend's BBQ as an offering. – Yumi

1 This is particularly good with a thick, artisan-style sourdough to soak up those tomatoey juices and bring a little extra flavour to the party.

2 I like to add the garlic to the tomato purée for a little extra kick, but if you prefer things less punchy – or if garlic doesn't agree with you – try rubbing a cut clove over the toast instead. When grating garlic, there's no need to peel it first, as the peel will get magically caught on the outside and won't make it through the holes. One less job to do!

COMMON COOKING MISTAKES AND FIXES

One of the most common mistakes people make when cooking is **going too slowly**. Just hurry up. Measure out the spoonful, tip it in, and then move on. A lot of people who don't cook much go into a kind of trance where everything slows down and they become ineffective somnambulistic underwater gobfish. I get that this is a leisure activity, but make sure you keep moving. Treat it like a job that you need to get done.

The same goes for **perfectionism when chopping**. Why does everything need to be cut into a perfect matching shape? Apples for a crumble, say, are going to turn into mush, hidden by a topping and then eaten with a spoon. It really doesn't matter. *Just chop the damn apple!* (Safely.)

Always start with a clean kitchen. It's a big mistake to try to cook in an **already messy kitchen** with a crowded sink and full dishwasher. Imagine an athlete at the starting line with a bunch of dirty frying pans tied to their waist. Shed the shit and become immaculate and unencumbered before the gun fires.

Calibrate your expectations. Make sure you have enough time to give your attention to the food. If **you don't have the time,** choose something simpler, quicker. Plan for the food to be ready by deciding on your serving time and working backwards. For instance, 'If we want to eat by 6 pm, and the potatoes take 45 minutes, then I need to have them in the oven by 5.15 at the latest.' If there's not enough time, cook something else.

Sometimes you might be tempted to **use ingredients that are past it.** Check your use-by dates. Some things last for ages – dried pulses, pasta, rice, kombu, salts. But oils, nuts, seeds and dairy can all turn, and when they do, they turn really evil. They can't be redeemed and they need to go in the bin or they'll ruin your dish.

One classic rookie error is getting halfway through a recipe and realising you're **missing a key ingredient**. We've said it before: if you're cooking from a recipe, read it all the way through before you begin.

And finally, a common error in home cooking is **under-seasoning.** Chefs in restaurants go hard on salt and sugar for a reason. Taste as you go, and make sure you're seasoning generously throughout the cooking process, of course bearing in mind that if you add too much you can't go back.

Emergency Tomato Sauce #2

SERVES 4–6 WITH PASTA

When you have a bag of tomatoes in the house and you don't know what to do with them, try this. The sauce is ready in the time it takes to get your pasta water boiling and the flavour is really something else – garlicky, tomatoey and fresh. I don't skin the tomatoes. They bring a ton of flavour, nutrition and even a bit of texture to the sauce, and I've never heard the kids complain. Life's too short to be skinning tomatoes.

It's important to cook this sauce over high heat – not only do you want it ready fast, but the tomatoes really benefit from cooking down quickly.

Heat the oil in a large frying pan over high heat. Add the garlic and let it sizzle and sputter for 1 minute until lightly coloured, then add the tomatoes. Stir well and bring to a vigorous simmer. Cook for 5–10 minutes, stirring often, adding a little pasta cooking water or boiling water as you go, until the tomato pieces have collapsed and formed a lovely thick, chunky sauce.

Season to taste with salt and pepper, then serve with your pasta of choice.

¼ cup (60 ml) extra virgin olive oil

6 garlic cloves, chopped

6–8 tomatoes, halved and roughly chopped into 1 cm (½ inch) pieces

a few splashes of pasta cooking water or boiling water

salt and pepper

If your tummy struggles with garlic, just don't add it. — Yumi

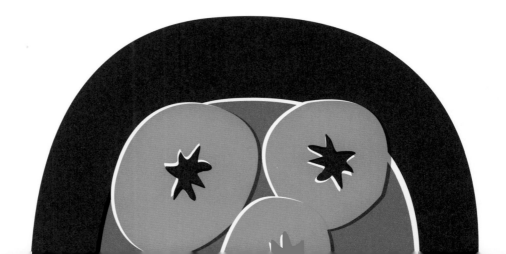

73

Yoshiko's Seaweed and Cucumber Salad

SERVES 6 AS A SIDE

⅓ cup (about 15 g) dried wakame seaweed

7 Lebanese (short) cucumbers (about 750 g/1 lb 10 oz)

1 tablespoon salt

¼ cup (60 ml) salad-quality white vinegar

2 teaspoons sugar

½ teaspoon soy sauce

My mum Yoshiko has always been a good cook. As she gets older, the amount she eats is shrinking – like her body – and the foods she's attracted to have evolved. She eats less and less meat, although she's still keen on seafood, and finds terrific enjoyment in the vast array of pickles, preserves and fermented foods from her home country, Japan.

Yoshiko has been making this salad since I was little. The wakame is easy to find and lasts an age in the cupboard, while she swears by the Aussie brand Skipping Girl vinegar. She would take this salad to Christmas lunch in an ornate glass bowl, and serve it alongside prawns, potato salad, onigiri and ham.

Soak the wakame in a bowl of cold water for at least 5 minutes. It will expand to four or five times its original size.

Meanwhile, trim the ends off the cucumbers, then cut into slices about 4 mm (³⁄₁₆ inch) thick. Pop in a bowl or jug (I use a large glass measuring jug). Sprinkle the salt over the cucumber and use your clean hands to toss and mix the salt through. Set aside while you make the dressing.

Mix the vinegar, sugar and soy sauce together in a separate small bowl or jug, stirring to encourage the sugar to dissolve.

Crush the cucumber slices in your hands, then give them a quick rinse by pouring over 1 cup (250 ml) of cold water, crushing them some more and draining the water off. You don't want to wash all the salt off, just dislodge a fair bit of it. Squeeze out as much of the moisture as you can. (You'll see a green, watery liquid come out, which is quite satisfying.) Drain the wakame, squeeze the liquid out of that too, then add it to the cucumber. Pour the dressing over the cucumber and wakame and mix well.

Taste it and adjust the seasoning as needed – it should be tangy, not painfully salty, and completely delicious, like an oceany, pickly salad.

TiPS

1 This has a pretty good afterlife in left-over heaven and makes a fantastic side to any rice-based lunch dish. It also goes great with potato salad.

2 Gluten-free soy sauce works perfectly well in this recipe.

Cold Noodle and Cucumber Salad

SERVES 4

200 g (7 oz) udon noodles

3–4 Lebanese (short) cucumbers, very thinly sliced

4 spring onions (scallions), thinly sliced

1 small bunch coriander (cilantro), leaves picked (optional)

½ cup (70 g) roasted peanuts, roughly chopped

salt (optional)

PEANUT DRESSING

½ cup (140 g) peanut butter

juice of 2 limes, plus extra as needed

¼ cup (60 ml) soy sauce or tamari

2 tablespoons sesame oil

2 tablespoons maple syrup

¼ cup (60 ml) water, plus extra as needed

2 teaspoons grated ginger

2 garlic cloves, grated

1 tablespoon chilli-garlic sauce (e.g. sambal oelek), optional

pinch of salt, plus extra as needed

I love it when I can pull together a salad primarily from pantry ingredients. And even more so when that salad can deliver crisp and cool, herby and bright notes. It's just the ticket for a hot summer's day, and the irresistible peanut and ginger dressing here makes this one nothing short of magic.

More than anything, though, I love this salad for its versatility: instead of cucumbers, udon noodles and coriander (cilantro), you can use any veg, herb and noodle – carrot, mint and soba, for example – as long as the veg is very thinly sliced.

To make the dressing, whisk together all the ingredients in a medium bowl. Taste and adjust with more lime juice or salt to taste. As the dressing sits, it may thicken. If so, add another 1 tablespoon water to thin it down.

Bring a large saucepan of water to the boil and cook the udon noodles following the packet directions. Drain and rinse under cold water.

Transfer the noodles to a large bowl, patting them dry with a clean tea towel if still necessary. Toss with ¼ cup (60 ml) of the dressing, then add the cucumber, spring onion, coriander, if using, and peanuts. Toss again. Taste. Add a splash more dressing and a little sea salt if needed, then serve immediately.

It slightly annoys me that Simon has such a good noodle recipe. WHO'S THE ASIAN HERE, BUDDY?! – Yumi

1. Left-over dressing will keep in an airtight container in the fridge for up to 2 weeks.

2. Use whatever peanut butter you have – chunky or smooth, big brand or natural label. Or you could use another nut butter if you prefer.

3. I like to use the mandoline that Yumi gave me to cut the cucumbers wafer thin, but if you don't have one (or you're nervous about losing your fingertips), just slice them as thinly as possible.

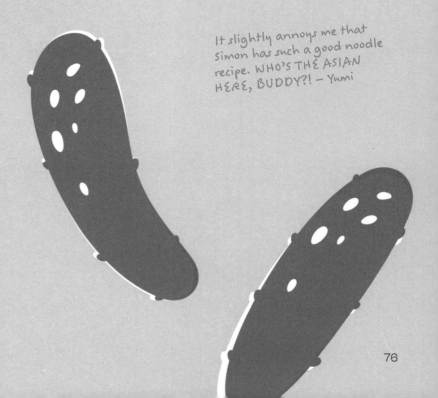

A Side of Burnished Broccoli

SERVES 3–4 AS A SIDE, OR 1–2 SMALL BOYS

I spent more than a year experimenting with broccoli, mainly as an ongoing and active expression of love for my son, who is a character, a laugh, an absolute punk and, at seven years old, a committed and passionate lover of broccoli, to the exclusion of all other vegetables.

Here's what I learned: 1. Broccoli is the GOAT vegetable. It's reliable, it's flavoursome, and it seems able to withstand supply chain, drought, flood and blight issues. 2. It's pretty hard to muck broccoli up. It's good under most circumstances, after most kinds of cooking. 3. The best way with broccoli is often the simplest. Like this one.

Chop the broccoli head into bite-sized florets. Halve the stem lengthways and slice it into half moons about 4 mm (³⁄₁₆ inch) thick. Put all the broccoli pieces in a ceramic or glass bowl and microwave on high for 1½ minutes.

Spread the broccoli out on a baking tray and drizzle with the olive oil. (You don't want to drown the broc in oil but you don't want to be excessively stingy either. I can confidently assert that you need about 1 tablespoon of oil but you're better off pouring it directly from the bottle than using a measuring spoon.) Sprinkle salt over the top and give all the pieces a little toss to coat them in the oil. Spread the pieces so none are overlapping.

Pop under the hot grill and cook, without turning, for 8–12 minutes. Keep an eye on them – depending on how hot the grill gets and how close the tray sits to the element, you may need less or more time. You'll also probably smell a nutty, burnt smell – a little of this is okay but watch that it doesn't burn. You want dark, crispy edges, and a golden burnish on some of the pieces.

Serve immediately.

300 g (10½ oz) broccoli

1 generous tablespoon best-quality olive oil

salt

1 The broccoli withers and fades as soon as it starts to cool. It doesn't look as good but it's still delicious. If you're putting together a lunch of leftovers, this is great in a bread roll with cheese and tomato, or on the side of a rice dish.

Grilled Asparagus with Mint and Cheese

SERVES 2 AS A MAIN, 4 AS A STARTER

This dish excites me. It's so yummy, it's so easy and everything in it tastes wonderful. The one tricky thing about it is that it's absolutely best eaten piping hot – so I would recommend being ready to eat before you pop it under the grill, and serving it direct from the baking tray.

Preheat the oven grill (broiler) to hot. Arrange the shelves so that your dish can sit about 12 cm (4½ inches) from the element.

Trim the asparagus by bending the spears until the woody ends snap off. Spread the spears out evenly in a single layer on a baking tray. Scatter the saganaki all over the asparagus. Zest the lemon over the asparagus. Scatter the slivered almonds over.

Pop under the grill for 5 minutes. Keep an eye on the asparagus: the corners of the cheese and the tops of the almonds should turn golden but not burn.

Meanwhile, quarter the zested lemon.

As soon as the asparagus is ready, whip it out, toss the mint over, squeeze one quarter of the lemon over the top, get it on the table and serve the rest of the lemon wedges on the side.

3 bunches of asparagus

200 g (7 oz) Greek saganaki cheese, grated

1 lemon

¼ cup (35 g) slivered almonds

1 small handful fresh mint leaves, chopped

As a bit of an asparagus purist, I wasn't expecting to love this as much as I did. It'd be great with basil instead of mint, too.
— Simon

TiPS

1. Asparagus is meant to be eaten with your bare hands. *Go forth and be a barbarian!*

2–3 bunches asparagus

juice of 1 lemon

2 tablespoons extra virgin olive oil

salt and pepper

40 g (1½ oz) parmesan or Grana
Padano cheese

1 small handful mint or basil leaves
(optional)

Asparagus and Parmesan Salad

SERVES 2–4 AS A SIDE

I could be fancy and call this a carpaccio, but I won't. It's just a very simple and delicious way with asparagus that preserves its fresh and minerally green flavour, tumbled together with the sparkle of citrus and the richness of parmesan cheese. For something raw and put together in a matter of seconds, it's very good indeed.

Trim the woody ends off the asparagus – the easiest way is to bend the spears until they snap and discard the bottom ends (or save them for making stock, page 103). Using a very sharp knife or a mandoline, cut the asparagus crossways into 2–3 mm (¾–1¼ inch) thick rounds. Keep the tips whole.

Combine the asparagus in a bowl with the lemon juice and olive oil. Season with salt and pepper and toss together well.

Arrange the asparagus on a large serving plate in an even layer. Using a vegetable peeler or grater, top the asparagus with shavings of parmesan or Grana Padano. Scatter the fresh herbs over, if using, and serve with plenty of crusty bread for mopping up the juices.

1. This is delicious as is, but if you want to turn it into more of a hefty offering, a soft cheese such as buffalo mozzarella or burrata would be lovely. Toasted pine nuts and/or some of Yumi's ridiculously good croutons (see page 204) would also be a nice touch.

2. This method also works well with zucchini (courgette). For a little pop of extra sweetness and to really scream spring/summer try adding some blanched frozen peas.

SAVING THE PLANET

ONE MANKY CARROT OR WITHERED BROCCOLI STEM AT A TIME

We all know we need to do more to look after this beautiful home of ours. (Let's face it, we've given her a pretty rough ride lately.) But what can we do about it in the kitchen?

The very best thing we can do for the environment is *use all the food we buy*. Sounds easy, but how do you make the most of what you've got?

Run down supplies so your fridge isn't crowded Not only will this give you room for new inspiration, but it will also deliver a ton of unexpected meals. Hoarding tinned foodstuffs (see page 16) may be good, fresh stuff less so.

Conduct a weekly fridge audit Check those use-by dates. Write in your calendar when things are due to go off. This may be deeply unsexy, but we both swear by the importance of this in having an idea of what needs using, when.

Lean into dishes that are natural fridge cleaners Stir-fried rice will happily accept a panoply of last-leg veg without complaint, while dishes that heavily feature roasted vegetables (such as the Rainbow Veg and Haloumi Tray Bake on page 94) can easily be adapted to use up pretty much anything you have on hand that would otherwise be destined for the bin. And remember, a frittata is your leftovers' best friend.

Get creative Think about how to use up those gnarly and strange bits and bobs. Broccoli stems? Chop them up and add to a stir-fry (or throw on the barbecue). Leftovers? Transform them into something remarkable. If inspiration doesn't strike immediately, a quick google should do the job, and if your enthusiasm for any of this is flagging, try to see it as a competition/attempt to unleash your inner nonna. Whatever works for you.

And if all else fails … COMPOST!

Broccoli Farfalle

SERVES 4–6

1 large head of broccoli, cut into small florets

2 garlic cloves

½ cup (125 ml) olive oil

salt and pepper, to taste

400–500 g (14 oz–1 lb 2 oz) farfalle

grated parmesan cheese, to serve

Set a fucking timer! – Yumi

Broccoli – not just a veg of champions (and about the only one both Yumi and I can consistently get our kids to eat) but also a delicious creamy pasta sauce? Sure thing! If you like a bit of heat and little ones aren't involved, then feel free to add a finely chopped fresh red chilli to the oil along with the garlic.

Throw the broccoli florets into a large saucepan of boiling salted water and cook for 8 minutes or until soft. Drain.

Squash the garlic cloves with the flat of a knife.

Heat the olive oil in a frying pan, then add the garlic and cook for 4–5 minutes, or until golden all over. Fish the garlic out of the pan and discard.

Add the broccoli to the pan and stir it around in the garlicky oil until well coated. Season generously with salt and pepper and keep it ticking away over medium–low heat for 10–15 minutes, squashing the broc with the back of a wooden spoon and adding a splash or two of water as necessary, so it all smooshes together to form a creamy sauce.

Meanwhile, cook the farfalle in a saucepan of salted boiling water until al dente.

Drain the pasta and add to the pan with the broccoli. Toss everything together and serve with plenty of grated parmesan and pepper.

1 Pasta always tastes better when it's cooked 'al dente' (which is just the Italian way of saying 'to the tooth' or that it has a bit of bite left in it). I tend to go by memory rather than timer – sorry, Yumi! – and taste mine as it cooks to see if it's just right, but if you're unsure then follow the packet directions, subtracting a minute or two as they always seem to be a bit cautious.

2 The pasta amount here is, well, variable because, let's be honest, it's almost impossible to cook the right amount. I tend to do this by eye or throw in a whole packet for a family of five. Any uneaten pasta makes good leftovers.

Korean Fried Cauliflower

SERVES 6–8

1 large, gorgeous head of cauliflower

1 cup (100 g) almond meal

½ cup (65 g) tapioca flour

200 ml (7 fl oz) tinned coconut cream

cooking oil spray

kewpie mayo and tonkatsu sauce
or just any peri peri or sriracha
sauce, to serve

SPICES

2 teaspoons ground white pepper

2 teaspoons salt

2 teaspoons garlic powder

2 teaspoons sweet paprika

2 teaspoons turmeric powder

2 teaspoons chilli powder (optional)

2 teaspoons cumin powder

ALTERNATIVE SPICES

100 g (3½ oz) good curry powder

I made these for a birthday party recently. They were snaffled up within a few minutes and everyone raved about them all night. But I also made them for a family Christmas and one of my cousin's daughters cried because the chilli burnt her mouth … Waah! Besides making small children cry, these delicious vegan treats rule. I love them on a bagel with avocado and sliced tomato, or cold the next day smooshed onto a cracker with cheese. Oh, and they're not actually fried.

The many spices in this recipe can be annoying, so I've included an excellent alternative that uses only curry powder.

Preheat the oven to 200°C (400°F).

Cut the cauliflower head into nugget-sized pieces. (You can also use the leaves and stem, cut into bite-sized pieces.) Spread the cauli over two baking trays and pop both in the oven for 15 minutes.

Meanwhile, combine the almond meal, tapioca flour and spices and whisk well to remove any lumps (I use the food processor for this).

Remove the cauliflower from the oven. Pour the coconut cream over the trays to coat the semi-cooked cauliflower, then scatter your magical powder over. You should have enough to coat the pieces all over, with maybe a little left over for next time. Spray lightly with cooking oil spray. Roast for 20 minutes or until charred and golden.

Serve with your choice of condiments.

My tip? Up the spices here and make those kids really cry. Delicious! — Simon

TIPS

1. Garlic powder can be a bit difficult to find and is not to be confused with granulated garlic, which is nasty. Look for it in greengrocers and Indian spice shops.

2. I often make double the crumbing mixture, label it and freeze it for next time.

3. Be aware that cauliflower shrinks down, so you might get less than you think.

4. Try this instead of, or in addition to, the black beans in the Black Bean Tacos recipe (page 43).

Roasted Capsicum and Cherry Tomatoes

SERVES 2 AS A MAIN OR 4 AS A SIDE

Summer food will always be my favourite sort of eating – easy breezy cooking, big flavours and food that doesn't chain you to the stove can be enjoyed at your leisure.

This classic Mediterranean combination screams sweetness, sunshine and good times. It's so simple to make, and is also ridiculously versatile. Chuck it in the oven and let it do its thing, then serve warm or cold as a starter for a fancy dinner, in the middle of the table with other bits and pieces as a side for a lunchtime barbecue feast or in a weeknight bowl with simply cooked rice (see page 32) or Yumi's Freakin' Fancy Pilaf (page 38). Job done.

Preheat the oven to 180°C (350°F).

Cut the capsicum in half lengthways with a sharp knife. Using your hand, pull out the seeds and white membrane, then use the knife to remove any left-over bits and pieces. (You will be left with a nice hollow capsicum half that looks like the hull of a small boat.) Place each half under running water to remove any remaining seeds, then pat dry with paper towel.

Transfer the capsicum halves to a large baking tray and place a few garlic slices inside each. Pile 2–3 cherry tomatoes, a few basil leaves and olives, if using, into each half and drizzle the olive oil and balsamic vinegar over everything. Season generously with salt and pepper.

Bake for 30–40 minutes, until the capsicum has softened and the cherry tomatoes have blistered and started to char. Remove from the oven and leave for a few minutes to cool, then transfer to a serving dish. Serve with crusty bread for mopping up the juices.

4 red capsicums (peppers)

2 large garlic cloves, thinly sliced

250 g (9 oz) cherry tomatoes

1 handful basil leaves

8 pitted kalamata olives, halved (optional)

1 tablespoon extra virgin olive oil

a drizzle of balsamic vinegar

salt and pepper

Bread is essential for the juice mopping. – Yumi

1. I like to vary these a bit with whatever I have to hand in the fridge and as the mood takes me – they're really good with a crumble of feta (or a few feta cubes marinated in olive oil) thrown into the mix, or with a scattering of toasted pine nuts over the top after cooking. (And if you don't have any fresh basil to hand, a little pesto, page 210, from the fridge works wonders here too.)

2. When I said these are versatile, I wasn't kidding! Along with the suggestions above, try them on a bed of hummus or tzatziki for a killer vegetarian main dish, or if you have leftovers, get out the kitchen scissors, throw everything in a bowl and chop roughly to make an instant flavour-packed pasta sauce.

Tomato Pie

800 g (1 lb 12 oz) tinned
   diced tomatoes

1½ cups (225 g) self-raising flour

1 teaspoon mustard powder

1 teaspoon salt

½ teaspoon ground white pepper

1 cup (100 g) finely grated Grana
   Padano cheese

½ cup (50 g) coarsely grated sharp
   and crumbly cheddar cheese

125 g (4½ oz) cold butter,
   cut into cubes

2 eggs

⅓ cup (80 ml) milk

a short squirt of sriracha sauce

6–8 ripe tomatoes, thinly sliced

SERVES 4–6

This recipe is a classic from Belinda Jeffery, a fantastic cook and food writer. I've been making it for years, and the combination of bright-tasting, joyous tomatoes and a cheesy, scone-like crust is so freakin' yummy it should probably be illegal.

Naturally I have made minor changes but I did not want to mess with perfection.

Preheat the oven to 180°C (350°F).

Decant the tinned tomatoes into a sieve over a bowl. Leave them to drain for 10–15 minutes while you make the crust, giving them an occasional stir to encourage as much liquid out as possible. (Catch the juice and freeze it for your next batch of chicken stock, page 103.)

Line the base of a 26 cm (10½ inch) round springform cake tin with baking paper and grease the sides with butter.

Measure the flour, mustard powder, salt and pepper directly into the bowl of a food processor. Whiz until well mixed. Add the cheeses and whiz again until just combined. Scatter the butter over the top, and process until the mixture resembles coarse breadcrumbs. (Sometimes I stop at this point and stash a container of this mixture, labelled, in the freezer for an emergency.) Transfer to a bowl.

In a medium jug or bowl, whisk together the eggs, milk and sriracha. Make a well in the cheese mixture and pour in the egg mixture, then stir everything together, being careful not to overmix. It should look like a shaggy scone dough.

Arrange the sliced tomato in a pattern on the base of the cake tin. Spoon the drained tinned tomatoes over the top and spread them out evenly.

Scrape spoonfuls of the cheese and egg dough onto the tomatoes and use your clean fingers to spread it out evenly. It doesn't have to be perfect.

Bake for 30–35 minutes, or until the topping has risen and is golden. Test it by sticking a skewer into the crust; if it comes out clean the pie is ready. Remove from the oven and leave it to rest for five minutes. Transfer the cake tin onto a large plate. Remove the sides and baking paper. Cut the pie into cake-like wedges to serve.

Hassle-free Oven Risotto

SERVES 4

I love, love, love risotto, but making it the traditional way can be an incredible pain – tip that rice into the pan and you've committed to 20 minutes of standing stove-side with no interruptions, constant stirring and loving ladling of stock. Given I normally have at least one child hanging off me at this point, this is no longer my idea of fun.

The solution? Why, bung it in the oven, of course! This recipe uses the oven to cook the pumpkin too, but it's really all about the method – once you've mastered it you can add whatever you like, safe in the knowledge that risotto is back on the menu.

Preheat the oven to 190°C (375°F) and line a baking tray with baking paper. Warm the stock in a small saucepan over low heat.

Roughly chop the unpeeled pumpkin and arrange in a single layer on the prepared tray. Drizzle half the olive oil over, season with salt and pepper, and bake for 30 minutes or until the pumpkin is soft but not mushy. Peel the skin off the pumpkin pieces and cut the flesh into rough cubes.

Meanwhile, warm the remaining olive oil in an ovenproof casserole dish that has a lid over medium–low heat. Add the onion and garlic and cook for 5 minutes, stirring occasionally, until softened, then add the rice and cook for 3 minutes, until the grains are evenly coated in the oil.

Add the wine and stir until it has been absorbed, then pour in the hot stock. Season with salt, stir everything together then put on the lid and transfer to the oven.

Bake for 20–25 minutes, until the rice has softened and the risotto is still a little liquid.

Add the pumpkin, rocket and olives, together with the butter and parmesan, and salt and pepper to taste, then stir everything together with a wooden spoon.

Ladle into bowls or onto plates and serve with a drizzle of olive oil and some extra grated parmesan.

4 cups (1 litre) vegetable or chicken stock

700 g (1 lb 9 oz) pumpkin (squash)

2 tablespoons olive oil, plus extra to serve

salt and pepper

1 onion, finely chopped

1 garlic clove, finely chopped

250 g (9 oz) risotto rice

150 ml (5 fl oz) white wine

2 handfuls rocket (arugula) leaves

12 pitted black kalamata olives, cut into quarters

1 tablespoon butter

2 tablespoons freshly grated parmesan cheese, plus extra to serve

1 I like to use roast chicken stock (page 103) if I have some lurking in the freezer, but if not, cartons of stock or even stock (bouillon) cubes or powder still give a great result.

2 And speaking of roast chicken, if you have some left over, it'll make a great addition to this risotto. Simply shred or roughly chop the meat and stir it through when you add the pumpkin, rocket and olives.

Cabbage and Peanut Salad

SERVES 4–6 WITH LEFTOVERS

Cabbage is both annoying and brilliant in that it takes so long to go off that it can sit in your crisper, occupying prime real estate, for months! Hopefully, having good use for this vegetable means that you'll actually get it out of the crisper and onto your plate. I'm always looking for ways that last night's dinner can be turned into next week's work lunch and this salad lasts wonderfully. Everything on the ingredients list is probably already in your pantry, and if you want to get fancy, you can add in a few optional extras.

Combine all the dressing ingredients, check for seasoning, adding salt if necessary, and set aside.

Shave or slice the cabbages as thinly as possible and place in a large mixing bowl. Core and slice the apples, rub with the lime halves to keep from discolouring, and add to the bowl.

Give the peanuts a quick whiz in the food processor to break them into smaller pieces (or chop them, or crush in batches using a mortar and pestle). Add to the salad, along with the carrot and mint, if using.

Mix all the salad ingredients together really well before pouring the dressing over.

DRESSING

100 g (3½ oz) peanut butter

juice of 1 lime (retain the lime halves)

2 tablespoons sesame oil

2 tablespoons rice vinegar

1 tablespoon neutral-tasting oil (e.g. grapeseed)

1 teaspoon finely grated fresh ginger (optional)

salt, to taste

SALAD

¼ white cabbage

¼ purple cabbage

2 green apples

1½ cups (210 g) toasted peanuts

1 large carrot, peeled and cut into thin matchsticks (optional)

1 large handful mint leaves, chopped (optional)

1. When you first start mixing the dressing, it will look like it won't integrate – but don't worry, it does.

2. If your kitchen doesn't have a fast turnaround of ingredients, it's worth checking that your peanuts and peanut butter haven't gone rancid. It happens, and it's gross.

Rainbow Veg and Haloumi Tray Bake

SERVES 2–4

2 zucchini (courgettes), cut into 2 cm (¾ inch) slices

1 red capsicum (pepper), cut into 2 cm (¾ inch) pieces

2 red onions, peeled and cut into thick wedges

1 sweet potato, cut into 2 cm (¾ inch) cubes

2 tomatoes, roughly chopped

1 garlic clove, finely chopped

2 tablespoons extra virgin olive oil

salt and pepper

chilli sauce (e.g. page 208), to serve (optional)

toasted flatbreads, to serve

HALOUMI

180–250 g (6¼–9 oz) haloumi cheese

1 teaspoon honey

1 teaspoon extra virgin olive oil

pinch of Aleppo pepper flakes (optional)

1. While it's not worth dying in a ditch over, Cypriot haloumi is definitely a cut above the supermarket rest flavour-wise, which isn't surprising really, given Cyprus is where haloumi comes from. If you can get hold of some easily (it tends to come in chunkier form), then give it a go. You won't look back.

2. I love the traditional drizzle of honey on the salty cheese, but you can always go with other flavourings instead – a little smoked paprika and a few fresh chopped thyme or oregano leaves make a lovely alternative too.

3. Aleppo pepper flakes, which can be found in specialty stores or online, have a distinct warm, zingy flavour, but ordinary chilli flakes or even chopped fresh chilli work well too.

Ah, the humble tray bake – best friend of all home cooks and busy parents for its easy assembly, and independent cooking.

This one has evolved over the years, but the ingredients usually depend on what's lurking in the crisper. Adapt it based on what you have, but follow these three basic principles: cut all the veg pieces roughly the same size (and any harder veg slightly smaller), don't overload the tray, and give everything an occasional shuffle around so it doesn't stick to the bottom.

Wrapping the haloumi in foil yields a lovely soft, tender cheese that's so much more delicious than if you threw it in the tray *au naturel*. Add hot sauce and toasted flatbreads for an extremely comforting midweek dinner.

Preheat the oven to 200°C (400°F).

Drain the haloumi and cut in half lengthways, then place on a square of foil. Drizzle the honey and olive oil over, scatter the chilli flakes over, if using, then tightly close up the edges of the foil to form a parcel. Set aside.

Combine all the vegetables in a large roasting tin. Drizzle the olive oil over, mix everything together well and season with salt and pepper, then roast for 20 minutes.

Check the vegetables, giving the pan a good shake and stir to make sure nothing is sticking to the base, then place the haloumi parcel on top and return to the oven for a further 20 minutes, or until all the vegetables are soft and nicely browned in places.

Remove from the oven, open up the parcel and pour the haloumi juices into the vegetables. Give everything a good mix together then divide between bowls and top with the haloumi as is or cut into cubes (depending on how many you are serving). Drizzle over a little of your favourite chilli sauce or Chilli Crisp Oil (page 205), if you like, and serve with toasted flatbreads.

Sounds too easy to believe it actually works! But it does and it's bloody great. — Yumi

Harissa Pumpkin with Pepita Sauce

SERVES 6

Pumpkin is a disrespected and under-appreciated quiet achiever, too rarely given leading-lady status. It could be that she doesn't cost enough, so we don't assign her any value; or that cutting pumpkin can be a pain in the ass; or that we assume it will take more than an hour to cook. But pumpkin is technically a fruit, a squash and a gourd, a shapeshifting and affordable fibre-rich friend that gets to well done in only half an hour.

Here's my favourite, quickest and easiest way to make pumpkin the main character. This recipe is easy to scale up, and the leftovers make for brilliant salad lunches or sandwich fillings.

Preheat the oven to 180°C (350°F).

Wash the pumpkin well because you're going to eat the skin. Slice it into wedges about 1.5 cm (⅝ inch) thick. Lay them out in a roasting tray and coat the upward-facing side in harissa paste, about 1 teaspoon per piece, so that they're generously covered. Sprinkle with salt and pepper, then drizzle the oil over everything. Pop them on the middle shelf of the oven and roast for 25–35 minutes.

Meanwhile, combine the pepitas, sultanas, salt and garlic in a food processor and whiz to fine crumbs. Add the yoghurt, honey and herbs and blend again until combined and saucy. Use a rubber spatula to scrape out the sauce – either into a small serving dish or (when it's done) directly onto the cooked pumpkin.

Check the pumpkin after 25 minutes. In my oven, the ideal cooking time for this dish is 35 minutes: you want the edges charred and the thickest part to be really, really well done. (It will be cooked through and soft at 20 minutes, but the additional 15 minutes really gets its sexy on.) It will depend on how hot your oven gets and your personal preference, so keep an eye on it and engage your senses.

Serve with the pepita sauce generously drizzled over.

800 g–1.2 kg (1 lb 12 oz–2 lb 10 oz) pumpkin (squash), skin on

50–75 g (1¾–2¾ oz) harissa paste

salt and pepper, to taste

¼ cup (60 ml) grapeseed or coconut oil

PEPITA SAUCE

¼ cup (40 g) pepitas (pumpkin seeds), toasted

2 tablespoons sultanas

½ teaspoon salt

½ teaspoon chopped or finely grated garlic

1 cup (260 g) plain or Greek-style yoghurt

1 teaspoon honey

2 tablespoons fresh herbs (e.g. tarragon, basil, mint, parsley)

Be liberal with the sauce here. It's the shit. – Simon

TIPS

1 You can use any variety of pumpkin except Golden Nugget (the Halloween pumpkin).

MEAT &

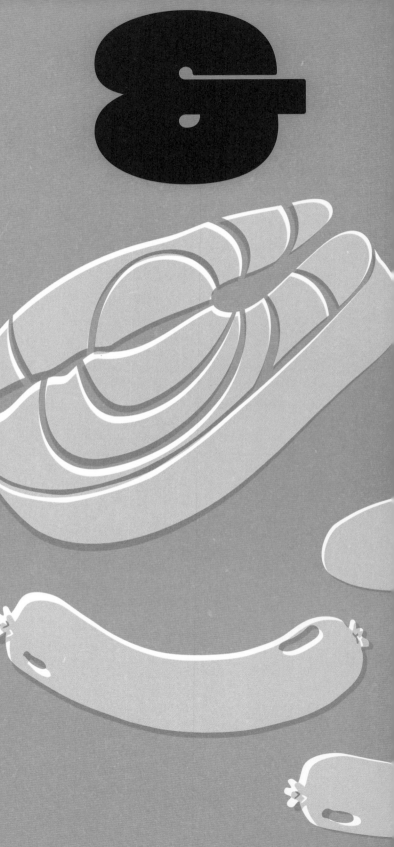

FISH

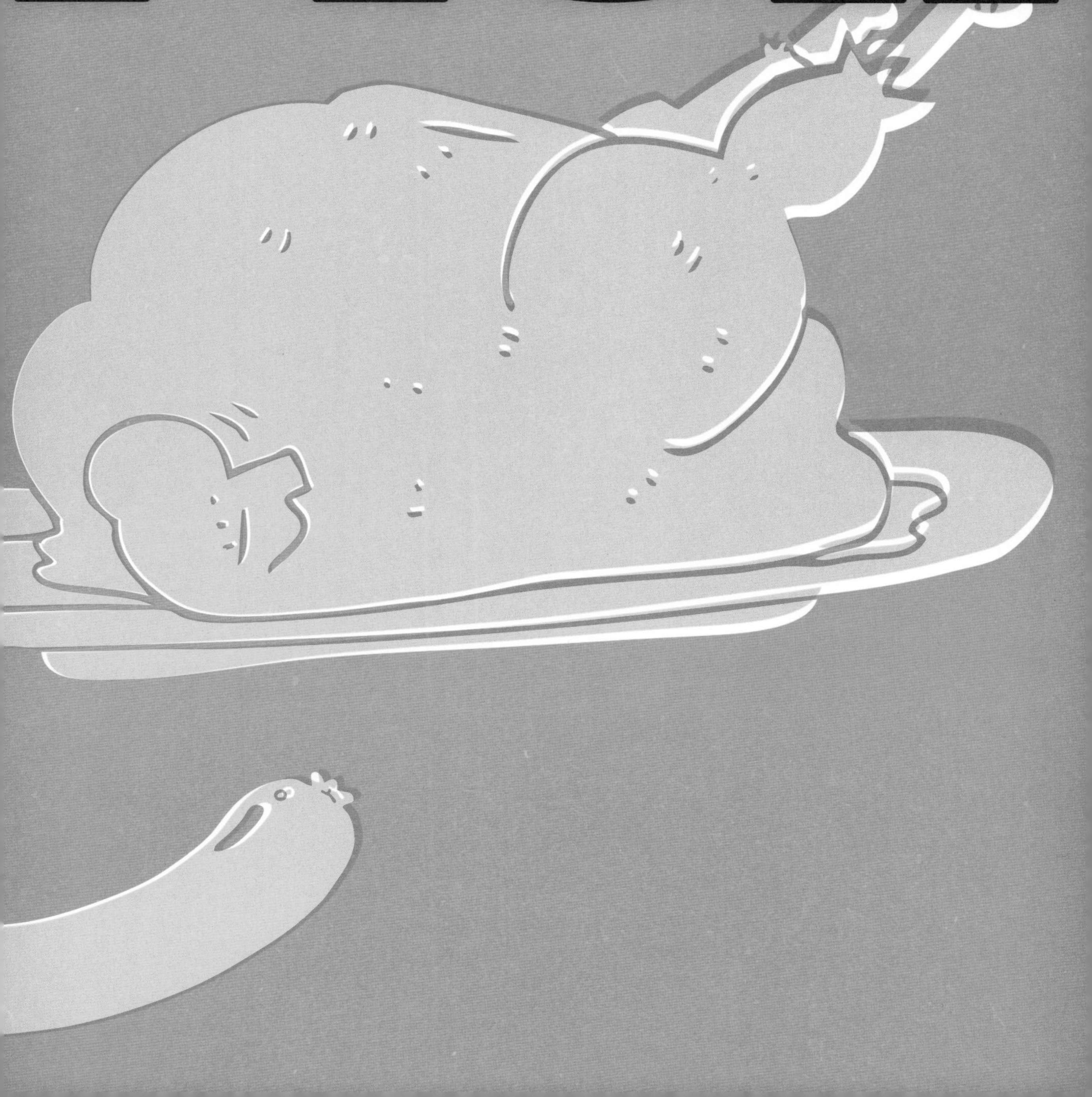

The Famous Chicken Wings

SERVES 8

1 garlic bulb, as fresh as possible, cloves separated and peeled, woody ends removed

1 thumb-sized piece (about 5 cm/ 2 inches) ginger, yucky bits trimmed, roughly chopped

3 long red chillies, seeded

¾ cup (260 g) honey

1 cup (250 ml) soy sauce

2 kg (4 lb 8 oz) halved and trimmed chicken wings (aka chicken wing nibbles)

When this recipe appeared in my first cookbook, my kids were all little and I was married. Now that I'm divorced (which, by the way, I highly recommend) and my kids are bigger, this dish is less about feeding my big family. These days I'll make it for friends who are going through a rough time, for any group whose principal cook is unwell, or when I'm having friends over and we want something that's as great fresh from the oven as it is later when the sun starts to sink in the sky. People still tell me they're the best chicken wings they've ever eaten.

Preheat the oven to 180°C (350°F). Line two large baking trays with foil and then baking paper.

Make a marinade by combining all the ingredients except the chicken in a food processor and blitz until everything is blended and smooth.

Arrange the chicken pieces on the prepared trays in one closely packed layer. (The corners of the pan get hotter, so I always place the thickest pieces of chicken there as they're less likely to burn.)

Pour the marinade over the chicken to coat it generously. You may not need all the marinade, in which case store it in a sealed glass jar in the fridge for up to 3 months.

Bake for 30 minutes, then turn and bake for a further 20 minutes. Turn one more time and cook for another 15–20 minutes. You want it lightly charred in places, so check it and maybe give it one more turn and another 15 minutes if necessary.

I like to serve it hot on steamed rice (page 32) or cold as part of a picnic or an office lunch.

Frankly, I'd like to be buried with these chicken wings. – Chrissie Swan

1 Chicken 'nibbles' are a version of wings sold in my local supermarket where the third joint is discarded and the other two parts of the wing are halved. I find them easier to handle and eat than wings. Wings may be cheaper and easier to come by, so definitely use them if you prefer.

Chicken and Sweet Potato Soup

SERVES 4–6

In the cycle and seasons of my kitchen, I feel the need to make chicken stock every couple of months. The smell can be a lot, though – to the point where I used to run an extension cord outside and cook it in the backyard in a slow cooker so I didn't have to spend all day breathing it in. I feel this need to make stock whenever I've run out, but also whenever the bag of stock scraps I keep in the freezer starts to get unmanageably full and I want to free up some space.

To make the stock, combine all the ingredients in a large stockpot over medium heat. Bring to the boil, then reduce the heat to low and simmer gently, covered, for 2 hours. Allow to cool, then strain and refrigerate in an airtight container. Once it's chilled, you should be able to skim the layer of fat off the top. Freeze or use within 4 days.

Pour the chicken stock into a large saucepan or medium stockpot and add the chicken breast. Place over medium heat and bring to a simmer.

Meanwhile, peel and dice the sweet potato (I cut mine into 5 mm/ ¼ inch dice – I find it comforting to have small, neat cubes in my soup). Make sure you've measured out the pasta and have it standing by. When the chicken breast is cooked (15–20 minutes), take it out with tongs and cut or shred it (I like small pieces almost dissolving into the soup, some like it torn along the grain in a satisfying shred, others like big chunks).

Return the chicken to the pot along with the sweet potato and the pasta. Cook for 5 minutes or until the sweet potato and pasta are cooked. Check for seasoning and add salt and pepper as needed.

Serve with Wedding-guest Croutons (page 204) or Two-ingredient Bread (page 47).

4 cups (2 litres) chicken stock

1–2 chicken breasts

1 sweet potato

½ cup tiny noodles (e.g. risoni, short-cut angel hair pasta, or spaghetti broken into 2 cm/¾ inch pieces)

1 teaspoon salt

½ teaspoon ground white pepper

CHICKEN STOCK

saved vegie scraps

2 carrots, snapped in half

1 onion, quartered

1 tablespoon stock/bouillon powder

1 teaspoon whole black peppercorns

1 fresh or dried bay leaf

1 teaspoon fennel seeds

carcass of 1 barbecued chicken, stuffing removed, or 1 kg (2 lb 4 oz) chicken wings/carcasses that have been roasted for 35 minutes at 180°C/350°F

16 cups (4 litres) water

1. My monthly vegie scraps might include tomato skins left over from making Pan Con Tomate (page 69), tomato juice from making Tomato Pie (page 88), onion/fennel/celery scraps, the woody ends of asparagus, stems from parsley and other herbs, parmesan rind, apple cores and carrot peel.

2. You can pad this out by adding milk and/or cream – just be careful not to boil the soup once it's been added, because it will split.

3. It can be tempting to overload a soup with chunky things like chicken and pasta, but don't forget that the broth should (and will) be delicious and needs space to express itself. Don't crowd it out of its own story.

Best-ever Roast Chicken

Yes, that's quite some title. But I stand by it. And you will too when you've given this one a whirl. This is a doddle to make; just plan ahead and spend two minutes getting the chicken in the brine the night before. The buttermilk tenderises the meat, adds flavour and helps the skin turn lovely and brown, while the salt and olive brine keeps things juicy and seasons the bird from the inside out. I've included a perfect side of potatoes, but it's totally optional, as is using olive brine (although I'm just glad to have found a use for it). Once you're done with the chicken, don't throw the leftovers in the bin. Turn over the page and make something marvellous instead.

Mix together the buttermilk, olive brine and salt.

Put the chicken in a large bowl or container and pour the brine mixture over, making sure the chicken is completely covered. Cover with plastic wrap or seal with a lid and refrigerate overnight.

An hour before you are ready to roast the chicken, remove it from the brine mixture and use a spoon to scrape as much of the mixture off it as you can. Discard the brine mixture. Pat the chicken dry with paper towel, then transfer it to a large roasting tray.

Preheat the oven to 210°C (410°F). Have a shelf ready in the middle of the oven with no shelves above it.

Halve the potatoes and arrange them around the chicken. Drizzle the olive oil over and season everything generously with salt and pepper.

Roast for 1 hour–1 hour 15 minutes, or until the juices run clear when a skewer is inserted into the thigh.

Meanwhile, mash the butter, olives and lemon zest together with a fork.

When the chicken is done, immediately remove it from the pan and rest it on a cutting board for 10–15 minutes before carving. Add the olive butter and the basil to the hot potatoes. Once the butter starts to melt, toss to mix everything together and serve.

1 cup (250 ml) buttermilk

1 cup (250 ml) olive brine, from any type of olives (if you don't have any, double the buttermilk)

pinch of salt (or 2 tablespoons if using buttermilk only)

1 whole chicken, about 1.75 kg (2 lb 12 oz)

OLIVE ROAST POTATOES

700 g (1 lb 9 oz) small new potatoes

2–3 tablespoons olive oil

salt and pepper

1 tablespoon butter, softened

6–8 pitted kalamata olives (or any pitted olives), finely chopped

finely grated zest of 1 lemon

1 small handful basil leaves, finely chopped

This is the only time anyone is allowed to say 'doddle' in a recipe. — Yumi

TIPS

1. Be sure to keep an eye on the chicken as it cooks. If it seems to be browning too quickly, cover it with foil for the remaining cooking time.

2. If you don't have any olives but have a surplus of pickled gherkins or cornichons, then try using these (and their brine) instead and perhaps replace the basil with something like parsley or dill.

LEFT-OVER ROAST CHICKEN

So you've made a beautiful roast chook and everyone's happy. What now? Here's what to do with what's left to turn one meal into many.

MAKE THIS

Roast Chicken Stock

Makes about 4 cups (1 litre) Using your clean fingers, strip the carcass of all remaining meat, setting it aside in an airtight container. Put the stripped carcass in a large saucepan together with 1 tablespoon salt, 1 peeled and halved onion, 1 halved carrot, 1 celery stalk cut into three lengths and a generous grind of pepper. Cover with 6 cups (1.5 litres) water and bring to the boil over high heat, then reduce the heat to low and simmer very gently for 1 hour. Strain the stock, discarding the bones and adding the spent vegetables to your compost. Chill in an airtight container in the fridge or freeze until needed.

AND THIS

Bang Bang(ish) Chicken Salad

Serves 2–4 Roughly shred the stripped chicken meat with clean hands and add it to a large bowl together with 1 Lebanese (short) cucumber cut into matchsticks, 1 grated carrot, 50 g (1¾ oz) sugarsnap peas or snow peas (mange tout) halved crossways, 3 finely chopped spring onions (scallions), 1 finely chopped fresh red chilli and 1 small handful coriander (cilantro) leaves. Whip up the Peanut Dressing from the Cold Noodle and Cucumber Salad recipe (page 76), pour into the bowl and toss everything together well. Serve topped with chopped roasted peanuts and lime wedges for squeezing.

OR THIS

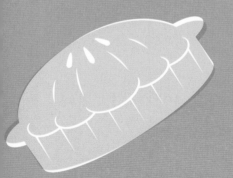

Easy as Chicken Pie

Serves 2–4 Heat 2 tablespoons olive oil in a large ovenproof frying pan over medium heat, add 2 thinly sliced onions and 1 teaspoon smoked paprika and fry gently for 10 minutes until lightly golden, then add 250 g (9 oz) frozen sweetcorn kernels, the stripped chicken meat, 200 ml (7 fl oz) crème fraîche, 200 ml (7 fl oz) chicken stock and 2 tablespoons finely chopped parsley. Bring everything to a gentle simmer, then remove from the heat. Lay 1 sheet of thawed frozen puff pastry over the top of the pan, securing the edges by pressing them down with your fingers, then brush the surface with a little beaten egg and bake in an oven preheated to 200°C (400°F) for 25 minutes, or until golden. Remove from the oven and set in the centre of the table on a heatproof mat to serve.

Chicken or Mushroom Karaage

SERVES 4

CHICKEN KARAAGE

500 g (1 lb 2 oz) chicken thigh fillets

100 g (3½ oz) karaage powder

4 cups (1 litre) oil for deep-frying
(I use rice bran oil or grapeseed oil)

MUSHROOM KARAAGE

500 g (1 lb 2 oz) button mushrooms

100 g (3½ oz) karaage powder

150 g (5½ oz) plain
(all-purpose) flour

4 cups (1 litre) oil for deep-frying
(I use rice bran oil or grapeseed oil)

TO SERVE

Cooked rice (page 32)

Japanese mayonnaise

tonkatsu sauce

whatever vegetables you have that
need to be used (here we used
tomato and cucumber; raw bok
choy, sliced carrot or roasted
broccoli are also good)

Yoshiko's Tsukemono
(page 215; optional)

1. You don't necessarily need to use
   a whole 100 g (3½ oz) sachet of
   karaage powder each time you make
   this. If you seal up the packet to
   make it airtight, it will last well in
   the pantry until you're ready to
   make this again.

2. The leftovers are great sliced up
   and put in an office bento-box-
   type lunch with rice, pickled ginger,
   Yoshiko's Tsukemono (page 215)
   and a boiled egg.

3. The most commonly found brand
   of tonkatsu sauce is Bull-Dog.

My two kids under ten demand Japanese-style chicken karaage once
a week. They call it 'favourite chicken', and in their eyes it's a flawless
meal. I'm glad it's reliable and delicious, but I'm also glad to have found
another way to keep it interesting for myself – by replacing the chicken
with mushrooms.

The whole point of this dish is to use store-bought crumbing mixture
(see the one I use in the pic on page 14, bottom left). If you're not lucky
enough to live near a good Asian grocer and you don't want to do an online
order, make the magical dust from the KFC cauliflower nuggets recipe
(page 84), omitting the paprika and almond meal but adding an extra
1 tablespoon ground ginger and 2 teaspoons onion powder.

Chicken karaage

Cut the chicken into nugget-sized pieces. Put the karaage powder in a
bowl and toss the chicken pieces in it to coat them well all over. Shake
off any excess and set aside on a plate.

Heat the oil in a large heavy-based saucepan or very stable wok over
medium–high heat. I usually test if the oil is hot enough by dipping the
end of a piece of chicken in. If it bubbles immediately in a lively fashion,
I know it's ready.

Using metal tongs, carefully lower the chicken into the oil three or four
pieces at a time. Give each piece about 4 minutes of total frying time,
turning it halfway. Remove using tongs and drain on a plate lined with
paper towel. Repeat until all the chicken is cooked. Serve immediately on
hot rice with Japanese mayo, tonkatsu sauce, cucumber, tomato and a side
of tsukemono pickles, if using.

Mushrooms karaage

For some reason the mushrooms taste excessively salty when fried
using the karaage powder on its own. Add the flour to the karaage
powder, mixing well, then add enough water to form a batter. Coat the
mushrooms in the batter.

Heat the oil in a large heavy-based saucepan or very stable wok over
medium–high heat. I usually test if the oil is hot enough by dipping
the end of a piece of mushroom in. If it bubbles immediately in a
lively fashion, I know it's ready. Using metal tongs, carefully lower the
mushrooms into the oil four or five at a time. They need about 6 minutes
to cook through and will be delicious – try one to see if it's cooked.

Serve immediately on hot rice with Japanese mayo, tonkatsu sauce,
vegetables and a side of tsukemono pickles, if using.

Sausage, Mustard and Basil Rigatoni

SERVES 4

Legendary English food writer Nigel Slater dreamed up this ingenious combination a good while back, and it has been delighting time-poor but flavour-loving non-Italians with its combination of some of Life's Best Things™ ever since.

When it's cold outside and I'm stuck in a pasta rut, I'll turn to this dish time and time again. It's creamy and comforting but packs a serious flavour punch, thanks to the herbs and spices in the sausages and the basil leaves stirred through just before serving. Jay, our podcast producer, who tried it the night after we talked about it on the show, gave it the thumbs-up and told us it was going on high rotation. As good as feedback gets.

Bring a large saucepan of salted water to the boil. Add the rigatoni and cook according to the packet directions until al dente.

Meanwhile, heat the olive oil in a large frying pan over medium–high heat. Squeeze the sausage meat out of the casings into the pan and cook, stirring and breaking up the meat with a wooden spoon into roughly walnut-size pieces as you go, for 5 minutes or until browned all over.

Add the wine and simmer for 5 minutes, scraping all the delicious browned bits from the bottom of the pan with the spoon, until reduced by about half, then add the cream, mustard and paprika, if using, and simmer for a further 2 minutes, until thickened and reduced slightly.

Remove from the heat, add the drained pasta and basil, and stir or toss together (if you're feeling brave) until everything is coated in the rich, creamy sauce. Pile into bowls and serve with grated parmesan.

I take huge jars of this sauce over to friends who are experiencing overwhelm. — Yumi

400 g (14 oz) rigatoni, medium shells or penne

1 tablespoon extra virgin olive oil

6–8 Italian sausages

¾ cup (185 ml) dry white wine

¾ cup (185 ml) thick (double) cream

3 tablespoons wholegrain mustard

pinch of smoked paprika (optional)

1 large handful basil leaves, roughly torn

grated parmesan cheese, to serve

1. The spices and flavours of Italian sausages really make this dish, so try to hunt them down if you can. If you're cooking this for kids or the heat-intolerant, you might want to look for simply flavoured ones without chilli, although this is one dish that does benefit from a tingle of heat. I've been known to use spicy Italian sausages and then add a few sprinkles of chilli flakes and a little drizzle of chilli oil at the end, too.

2. If the flavours here appeal but everything is sounding a bit too rich for your tastes, this can be made a lot lighter surprisingly easily, without sacrificing flavour. Just replace the cream with 3 tablespoons low-fat cream cheese and ⅓ cup (80 ml) semi-skimmed milk, and the wine with ¼ cup (60 ml) vegetable or chicken stock.

Japanese Pork Belly in Toffee

MAKES 12 SMALL PORTIONS

500–900 g (1 lb 2 oz–2 lb) piece
of pork belly

1 brown onion, cut into 4–5 pieces

2 garlic cloves, peeled and halved

1 thumb-sized piece (about 5 cm/
2 inches) ginger, sliced

TOFFEE

¼ cup (60 ml) soy sauce

⅓ cup (80 ml) mirin (sweet rice wine)

1 teaspoon sugar

1 small (about 2 cm/¾ inch)
piece of ginger

This rich, sweet pork is intended to be eaten in small portions as an accompaniment to other dishes like rice and pickles, or as part of a bento, or lovingly laid on top of a ramen soup. The cooking process is almost a type of preservation so the pork will last a long time in the fridge (upwards of a week), and can also be frozen and used when required. Any kind of pork belly is rich, so don't eat too much of it! But enjoy this almost like a condiment with an otherwise vegetarian meal.

Slice the pork belly into pieces that will look lovely on a bowl of rice; I make mine about 1.2 cm x 7 cm (½ x 2¾ inches).

Put the pork, onion, garlic and ginger in a large saucepan and cover with cold water. Bring to the boil over medium heat. Reduce the heat slightly if necessary and cook for 1 hour with the lid of the saucepan slightly open. Top up the water if it looks like it's boiling dry.

Drain off the cooking liquid, retaining 400 ml (14 fl oz), and transfer the pork only to a clean saucepan or wash the old one. The onion, garlic and ginger can be composted.

Add the toffee ingredients and the retained cooking water to the pork, place over low heat and bring to a gentle simmer. Cook with the lid on for another 50 minutes.

After 50 minutes, remove the ginger (which can develop a bitter flavour if overcooked), then cook with the lid off for another 30 minutes. The sauce will reduce and turn into a glossy liquid toffee. Be careful not to burn it in the last 10 minutes.

I like to serve this pork with rice, as a side with onigiri or tucked into a bento box.

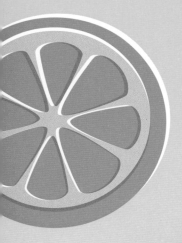

Tofu-skin Pork Rolls

SERVES 4–6

100 g (3½ oz) shiitake mushrooms

200 g (7 oz) enoki mushrooms

75 g (2¾ oz) sliced water chestnuts

500 g (1 lb 2 oz) minced (ground) pork

1 tablespoon grated fresh ginger

1 teaspoon ground white pepper

3 tablespoons thinly sliced spring onion (scallion), green tops only, plus extra to serve

1 tablespoon soy sauce

125 g (4½ oz) tofu skin sheets or spring roll wrappers

2 tablespoons neutral-tasting oil (e.g. grapeseed, canola, sunflower), for frying

toasted sesame seeds, to garnish

SAUCE

1 tablespoon cornflour (cornstarch)

2 tablespoons oyster sauce

1½ teaspoons sesame oil

1½ cups (375 ml) water

1½ teaspoons salad-quality white vinegar

The thing I love about this recipe is that it demystifies the meat-rolled-up-in-pastry treat we order at yum cha but feels out of reach at home. It's not tricky, and works on the principle of an achievable protein filling and a contrasting dipping sauce. Tofu skin, as a wrapping ingredient, is incredibly forgiving and bendy, and also way healthier than spring roll pastry. It makes for a chewy, succulent finish. If you can't find tofu skin, though, mainstream supermarkets carry spring roll wrappers in their freezer section – use those instead and skip the sauce. The finish will be crunchy and fantastic.

Finely chop the shiitake and enoki mushrooms and the water chestnuts.

In a large bowl, mix the pork with the ginger, white pepper, spring onion, soy sauce and chopped mushrooms. Use your clean hands to mix well.

Cut the tofu skin sheets into 15 cm (6 inch) squares – they don't have to be perfect and can be as raggedy and uneven as you like. Save the offcuts for a stir-fry, or to add to ramen (page 20) or udon (page 25). If you're using spring roll wrappers, have them standing by, lightly covered with a clean tea towel so they don't dry out.

Place a sausage of pork mix diagonally across the middle of a tofu-skin square and fold in the edges at each end of the sausage before rolling up to close. Repeat until all the mixture is used. You should make about 16 rolls of about 55 g (2 oz) each. Refrigerate in an airtight container until needed. (They will last 3 days if well refrigerated, and won't stick together if you're using tofu skin. If you're using spring roll wrappers and you're not cooking them right away, they will absolutely stick together. Spread them out on a tray so they're not touching before popping them in the freezer. Fry them from frozen.)

To make the sauce, combine the cornflour, oyster sauce and sesame oil in a jug. Add enough water, a little at a time, to create a slurry and dissolve the ingredients, then add the remaining water and the vinegar, and mix well.

To cook, heat the oil in a large frying pan over medium–high heat. Fry the tofu rolls, seam side down, for 2–3 minutes, then turn and cook the other side for 2–3 minutes, until cooked through and looking sealed and delicious. Remove and set aside. Add the sauce mixture to the frying pan and stir vigorously. As soon as it starts to boil you'll see it thicken to a glossy sauce. At this stage return the tofu rolls to the pan and warm them through, coating them well in the sauce. Remove to a plate, garnish with spring onion greens and sesame seeds, and serve immediately.

1. Tofu skin sheets are also sold as yuba sheets.

2. Yes, the rolls are in a sauce already, but you can also add a dipping sauce if you want.

Lamb Tacos with the Works

SERVES 4–6

When I do go for red meat, it tends to be like this – where the meat is special but only forms part of the overall show. The sweet lean meat is a real hit with the little ones, and there's tons going on flavour-wise, while the choose-your-own-adventure nature of this dish always goes down well. For vegies, try roasting up some chunks of capsicum, zucchini (courgette) and eggplant (aubergine) in the same spice mix. I defy you not to fall in love with the beetroot borani here – it's so pretty, so easy to whip together and so, so delicious.

Place the lamb in a large bowl. Drizzle the vegetable oil over, sprinkle with the Mexican spice mix and combine well. Season generously with salt and set aside for 10–15 minutes to come to room temperature.

If making the quick-pickled onions, do so now and put them in a serving bowl. Put the cabbage and avocado in their own serving bowls.

To make the beetroot borani, rinse the beetroot, then put it in a food processor with the yoghurt, lemon juice and salt. Give everything a quick pulse so that the ingredients are combined but the beetroot still has a little texture to it. Spoon the mix into a serving bowl and top with the mint leaves. Set aside.

To make the sweetcorn salsa, drain the corn and put it in a serving bowl with the smoked paprika, olive oil, coriander and salt. Mix together well.

Meanwhile, preheat a barbecue grill to medium–high or a grill pan over medium–high heat.

When ready to cook the lamb, place it on the preheated barbecue grill or on the grill pan and cook for 2–3 minutes on each side until nicely charred. Remove from the pan and leave to rest for 5 minutes, then cut into thin slices and transfer to a serving bowl. Drizzle olive oil over and season with salt and pepper.

While the lamb is resting, warm the tortillas on the barbecue or griddle pan, or in the microwave according to the packet directions, until soft and pliable.

To serve, place two tortillas on each plate. Put all the other ingredients in their bowls in the centre of the table, together with the lime wedges for squeezing and your favourite chilli sauces and other condiments, then invite everyone to help themselves.

500 g (1 lb 2 oz) lamb backstrap

2 tablespoons vegetable oil

2 teaspoons Mexican spice mix

salt and pepper

1 batch of Quick-pickled Red Onions (page 214) or 1 red onion, halved and thinly sliced

¼ small red cabbage, sliced

1 avocado, sliced

olive oil, for drizzling

8–12 small corn tortillas

2 limes, cut into wedges

chilli sauce (e.g. page 208) and other condiments, to serve

BEETROOT BORANI

300 g (10½ oz) cooked beetroot

¼ cup (70 g) Greek-style yoghurt

juice of ½ lemon

salt

1 handful mint leaves, finely chopped

SWEETCORN SALSA

420 g (14¾ oz) tinned sweetcorn

1 teaspoon smoked paprika

2 teaspoons extra virgin olive oil

1 handful coriander (cilantro) leaves, plus extra to serve

generous pinch of salt

1 Beetroot borani is a traditional Iranian mezze dish usually made with fresh beetroot that have been boiled or roasted until soft. You could use these, or buy pre-cooked packaged beetroot from the supermarket.

2 If you can find authentic corn tortillas (made with nixtamalised corn) you'll notice a massive difference in both flavour and texture. Try selected supermarkets or online.

Best-ever Bolognese

SERVES 12 COMFORTABLY, WITH LEFTOVERS

2 tablespoons extra virgin olive oil

1 parmesan rind

1 rosemary sprig, leaves picked
and finely chopped

1 large onion, finely chopped

2 garlic cloves, finely chopped

2 carrots, finely chopped

2 celery stalks, finely chopped

1 red capsicum, finely chopped

4 rashers smoked streaky bacon,
finely chopped, or 1 tablespoon
Bacon Jam (page 209)

1 kg (2 lb 4 oz) minced (ground)
beef or minced pork and veal

1 cup (250 ml) red wine

1.2 kg (2 lb 10 oz) tinned
chopped tomatoes

1 cup (250 ml) tomato passata
(puréed tomatoes) or water,
if required

a few dashes of Worcestershire sauce

a few dashes of soy sauce

1–2 teaspoons tomato ketchup
or mushroom ketchup

1 square of very dark chocolate
(minimum 75% cocoa solids)

salt and pepper

Obviously, pretty much everyone in the world has their own take on what makes a great spag bol, but this is mine. Yes, there are some little oddities here that might make it read a bit like Roald Dahl's *George's Marvellous Medicine*, but they all come together to form a mesmerising symphony. They're also all pretty much optional. What isn't, is making this in quantity. Given the time it takes and the fact that bolognese tastes so much better the next day, there's really no point not making a large batch. And *that's* before you've even turned the page to see all the fantastic things you can do with the leftovers …

Heat the oil in a large saucepan, casserole dish or stockpot over medium heat, then add the parmesan rind and rosemary. When the rosemary starts to sizzle, add the onion, garlic, carrot, celery and capsicum. Reduce the heat to medium–low and cook for 15–20 minutes, stirring occasionally to stop the parmesan sticking to the bottom of the pan, until the vegetables are super soft and tender.

Using a slotted spoon or spatula, remove the vegetables and parmesan from the pan and set aside in a bowl. Increase the heat to medium–high, add the bacon to the pan and cook for 2–3 minutes, stirring constantly, then add the beef and cook until browned all through.

Increase the heat to high, return the vegetables to the pan, mix everything together well, then pour the red wine over. Bring to a vigorous simmer and cook, stirring frequently, for 5–10 minutes, until all the wine has evaporated, the meat is glossy and your kitchen smells like heaven. Add the tomatoes and bring to a simmer, then reduce the heat to very low and leave to putter away for 2–3 hours, adding the passata or water if it looks like it's in danger of drying out, until the sauce is thick and unctuous.

Now for the fun bit. Taste the sauce, then add a dash or two of Worcestershire sauce and soy sauce and a tiny dollop of ketchup. Taste again – you're looking for a balance of sweetness and tomatoey richness from the ketchup with the saltiness and intensely savoury notes of the Worcestershire and soy sauces. When you feel you have the perfect balance, add the dark chocolate, give it a stir to let it melt through, then taste again. Magic, huh? If you think it needs it, season with salt and pepper to taste before you remove it from the heat. Job done.

If you've made a big batch or are saving it for tomorrow, it will keep in an airtight container in the fridge for 4 days or the freezer for 3 months.

BEST BOLOGNESE is like saying 'I'm the best looking'. You're probably NOT. Lol. Bold claim, but I like it! – Yumi

1. If serving with spaghetti, be sure to stir the sauce through rather than plonking it on top of the pasta like a comedy hat. A heavy showering of parmesan or Grana Padano is also non-negotiable.

LEFT-OVER BOLOGNESE

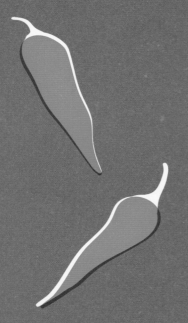

Making a big batch of bolognese (page 118) saves time and will make Future You a much happier person. Here's some ways you can use it ...

MAKE THiS

Chilli Con Carne

Serves 4 Add a 400 g (14 oz) tin of drained kidney beans, a few finely chopped long red chillies, a chopped red capsicum or two, a pinch or two of smoked paprika and a good splash of Tabasco to 400 g left-over bolognese. Cook in a saucepan for 5–10 minutes to warm through. Serve with shredded iceberg lettuce, chopped tomato, a little grated cheese and sour cream, in tacos or dolloped on nachos.

Cottage Pie

Serves 4–6 Warm 600 g left-over bolognese and pour into a small baking dish so the sauce is at least 2.5 cm (1 inch) deep. Cover with a layer of frozen peas and stir through the sauce to mix evenly, then top with mashed potato. Bake in a preheated 200°C (400°F) oven for 20 minutes until bubbling and golden.

Stuffed Capsicums

Follow the instructions on page 87 to prepare the capsicums, but instead of filling with tomatoes, olives and the rest, spoon left-over bolognese into the hollowed-out halves (if you've got some, a bit of left-over rice would be great here too). Sprinkle with grated parmesan cheese and bake in a preheated 200°C (400°F) oven until the filling is hot and the top is dark, golden and bubbly.

Other uses? There are tons. Try using bolognese to top a baked potato. Or in a pasta bake. Or (if you're feeling adventurous), stuffing a little into balls of left-over cooked risotto, then covering in breadcrumbs and shallow-frying to make crispy arancini. Finally – and my favourite – use a little warmed bolognese to top a slice of sourdough toast. Shower generously with grated parmesan, drizzle with balsamic vinegar and finish with a few good grinds of black pepper and you've got the perfect fridge-raid meal for one.

Credit-crunch Steak

SERVES 4

During the 2008 global financial crisis, our enterprising butcher encouraged customers to opt for cheaper but no less delicious cuts with this crafty bit of rebranding. Known as flat-iron steak in the US and butler's or feather-blade steak in the UK, this cut comes from the chuck and is cut with the grain, giving it a fantastic texture and a similar juiciness and depth of flavour to its more expensive cousins. If you can't find it easily, do a quick online search, hassle your butcher to stock it or use oyster blade steak instead.

To make the anchovy butter, if using, combine all the ingredients in a medium bowl. Mix well with a fork until smooth. Transfer to the centre of a large square of baking paper, roll up into a cylinder and chill in the fridge until ready to serve.

For the chimichurri, if using, put all the ingredients except the salt and pepper in a food processor. Pulse together briefly so that the herbs retain some texture but everything is well combined. Season to taste with salt and pepper and set aside.

Remove the steak from the fridge and lay it on a plate. Season generously with salt on both sides and set aside for 10–15 minutes to come to room temperature.

Preheat a barbecue grill to medium–high or a grill pan over medium–high heat. Grill the steaks for 3–4 minutes on each side or until cooked to your liking. Transfer to a large plate or serving platter.

If you've made the anchovy butter, use it all to top the steaks. Either way, loosely cover the steaks with foil and leave for 5 minutes to rest.

When ready to serve, transfer the steaks to a cutting board and slice thinly against the grain, then return to the platter and dredge in the juices (buttery or otherwise). Drizzle the chimichurri over, if using, and serve with your choice of sides – I vote for a well-dressed green salad and a bronzed, burnished baked potato.

Anchovy butter is sexier than lingerie IMHO. – Yumi

4 x 170 g (6 oz) flat-iron (chuck) steaks

salt

ANCHOVY BUTTER (OPTIONAL)

125 g (4½ oz) unsalted butter, softened

4 garlic cloves, crushed

8 anchovies in extra virgin olive oil, drained and finely chopped

½ teaspoon smoked paprika

½ teaspoon lemon juice

salt, to taste

1 tablespoon finely chopped flat-leaf parsley leaves

1 tablespoon finely snipped chives

CHEAT'S CHIMICHURRI (OPTIONAL)

1 small handful flat-leaf parsley, leaves picked

½ cup (20 g) oregano leaves

finely grated zest and juice of 2 lemons

¼ cup (60 ml) extra virgin olive oil

4 garlic cloves, crushed

2 teaspoons apple cider vinegar

salt and pepper

1 More than most steaks, flat-iron really benefits from being cut against the grain – that is against the direction in which the muscle fibres run. Look for these (don't get them confused with the grill marks on the surface of the meat) and cut in the opposite direction into nice thin slices to end up with tender steak rather than something that tastes like a rubber band.

BURGERS

It's only recently that I've really understood how excellent a good burger can be. I think before then I hadn't really had a proper, decent burger. I had had something approximating a warm meat sandwich – which sounds like a metaphor for bad sex and wasn't right and DID NOT SPARK JOY. Here are Simon's top three tips on making a really enjoyable and delicious burger at home.

1.

Choose the Right Meat

It's worth going the extra mile for nice beef mince. Pick up a combo of chuck and flank from your butcher if you can – it has a great fat/meat ratio that means you won't need to add anything else to it except salt and pepper.

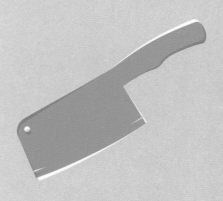

2.

Get Your Buns Right

Choose the right buns for the job! Don't go for brioche if you don't like things sweet, and if you like a soft floury roll then opt for that. Whatever you choose, be sure to toast your bun halves lightly before you put the burger together – it'll take things to that next level flavour-wise and create a slight barrier so that all the juices don't just soak straight into the bread and turn it to mush.

3.

The Other Bits

A burger's always better when you get to build it just the way you like it, so put out bowls of tomato slices, lettuce leaves, pickles, onions and the rest on the table and let everyone do it themselves! And if you've got any requests for cheeseburgers, be sure to put the slices on top of the patties for the last minute or two of cooking to let the cheese melt into them.

Baked Fish, Fennel and Olives

SERVES 4

500 g (1 lb 2 oz) potatoes, cut into 5 mm (¼ inch) slices

4 small fennel bulbs, trimmed, cored and thickly sliced lengthways, fronds reserved

¼ cup (60 ml) extra virgin olive oil

salt and pepper, to taste

4 skinless and boneless white fish fillets (e.g. barramundi, dory, ling)

1 teaspoon fennel seeds, crushed

1 spring onion (scallion), thinly sliced

2 tablespoons white wine vinegar

2 tomatoes, diced

1 small handful basil leaves, chopped

1 small handful drained pitted black olives, halved

This is great to serve straight from the tray. — Yumi

A simple all-in-one fish supper. I love the way that baking fennel like this caramelises it until it's soft and sweet – the perfect counterpoint to the salty olives and fruity, herby dressing. Be sure to save the fennel fronds to use as a garnish on the finished dish here. To bin them would be a huge waste – not only do they look pretty, but they bring lots of extra flavour to the party.

Preheat the oven to 200°C (400°F).

In a large baking dish, toss the potatoes and fennel with 1 tablespoon of the oil. Season with salt and pepper, then spread in a single layer and bake for 20–25 minutes, or until golden and nearly cooked through.

Place the fish on top, sprinkle with the fennel seeds and season again. Bake for another 10 minutes, or until the fish is cooked through.

Meanwhile, make the dressing. Put the spring onion in a small bowl, pour the vinegar over, then set aside for 2–3 minutes. Add the tomatoes, basil, olives and remaining olive oil, then season and mix together.

As soon as the fish, fennel and potatoes are ready, pour the dressing over, scatter with the fennel fronds and serve.

Heaps-Aussie Tuna Crudo

12 wonton or spring roll wrappers

neutral-tasting oil, for deep-frying

1 Lebanese (short) cucumber

½ ripe but firm avocado

2 red bullet chillies

2 tablespoons finely chopped
coriander (cilantro)

150 g (5½ oz) sashimi-grade tuna

1 tablespoon mixed black and white
sesame seeds, toasted

DRESSING

1½ tablespoons Japanese soy sauce

1 tablespoon mirin (sweet rice wine)

2 tablespoons lime juice

1 teaspoon sesame oil

*Heaps Aussie = heaps good.
Maybe avocado should be
added to everything after all?
— Simon*

 TiPS

1. Add a couple more chopped chillies
   to the left-over dressing and sit
   it on the table so people can help
   themselves. Or store the extra
   dressing in an airtight container
   in the fridge for up to 2 weeks.

2. Spring roll wrappers are easier to
   fry than wonton wrappers which
   make the oil spatter. Both have
   a subtle flavour that doesn't jostle
   for attention with the crudo but they
   add a lovely crunchy texture and
   act as a sort of spoon. If you don't
   have either of these (you may have
   leftovers if you've made Tofu-skin
   Pork Rolls, page 114, or gyoza, page
   173), then just use lettuce or endive
   leaves, or prawn crackers.

SERVES 4

Becoming confident with raw seafood can take time, but if you always serve it the same day you buy it, you'll be fine. Decide as you shop whether it looks fresh enough, and if you don't like the look of it, don't buy it. I nerdily shop for fish with a cooler bag and two ice bricks, to keep the seafood cool on the trip home.

The raw tuna is very gently cured in a little bit of lime juice and soy sauce here. Simon laughs at my heaps-Aussie tendency to add avocado to everything, but I love that it can hang back in flavour while adding vegan fattiness.

Combine the dressing ingredients and set aside. If you can't be bothered making the dressing, store-bought roasted sesame dressing (e.g. Kewpie brand) does a great job.

Cut the wonton or spring roll wrappers into triangles. Heat the oil in a large heavy-based saucepan or very stable wok over medium–high heat. Test if the oil is hot enough by dipping the end of a piece of wonton or spring roll wrapper in. If it bubbles immediately in a lively fashion, it's ready. Using metal tongs, carefully lower the wonton or spring roll wrapper pieces into the oil and deep-fry them in small batches, then set them aside.

Trim the ends off the cucumber then halve it lengthways. Use a teaspoon to scrape the seeds out (eat or compost these). Finely dice the cucumber. Do the same with the avocado but chop into larger dice. Finely chop the chillies, seeding them if you don't like heat. Mix the chopped vegetables together in a large bowl with the coriander, then carefully cut the tuna into a neat dice and add it to the bowl.

Combine everything gently, add about half the dressing, then taste. You may want more dressing, but this may be enough. (If using store-bought sesame dressing, just 2 tablespoons should be plenty.) Scatter the sesame seeds over the top to serve.

Eat it by spooning a teaspoonful onto a deep-fried wonton or spring roll wrapper and eating with your hands.

Salmon with Horseradish Yoghurt

SERVES 2

Poaching delivers a virtually idiot-proof path to perfectly cooked fish, keeping the flesh lovely and moist. That it also results in minimal clean-up and keeps fishy aromas to a minimum is no bad thing either.

Sydney-based fish chef genius Josh Niland makes a compelling case for serving yoghurt-based sauces with fish in place of the usual lemon. This one here takes seconds to put together and its punchy creaminess really complements the richness of the salmon (or you could use ocean trout instead). Serve with Quick Italian Roast Potatoes (page 51) and something green, and you're onto a winner.

Combine the wine, bay leaves, peppercorns, lemon, stock cube and water in a saucepan and bring to the boil over medium heat.

Remove from the heat. Slowly lower the salmon fillets, skin-side up, into the poaching liquid, then cover with a lid and leave to cook in the residual heat of the water for 10 minutes. Do not be tempted to check on it – you want to keep all the heat in there and let the salmon do its thing. The salmon will still be a little pink in the centre just the way I like it, but if you like yours cooked all the way through, then give it another couple of minutes.

While the salmon is poaching, make the horseradish yoghurt by mixing all the ingredients together in a bowl.

Using a spatula, carefully remove the salmon fillets from the poaching liquid and place skin-side up on a plate or work surface. Leave to rest for 2 minutes, then gently peel away the skin (if it comes off easily then you'll know the fish is properly cooked; if it doesn't, bring the water back to the boil, remove from the heat, and pop the salmon back in the water for another minute or two). Divide the fish between two plates, drizzle a little extra virgin olive oil over and finish with a sprinkling of salt and a few grinds of black pepper. Serve with spoonfuls of the horseradish yoghurt and quick Italian roast potatoes and burnished broccoli or your choice of sides.

I taught Simon everything he knows about fish. — Josh Niland

½ cup (125 ml) white wine

2 fresh bay leaves

1 tablespoon black peppercorns

1 lemon, thinly sliced

1 vegetable stock cube

8 cups (2 litres) water

2 x 200 g (7 oz) salmon fillets, skin on

extra virgin olive oil, for drizzling

Quick Italian Roast Potatoes (page 51), to serve (optional)

A Side of Burnished Broccoli (page 77), to serve (optional)

HORSERADISH YOGHURT

½ cup (130 g) Greek-style yoghurt

1 tablespoon horseradish cream

1 teaspoon extra virgin olive oil

salt and pepper, to taste

1 I like to add the bay leaves, peppercorns and lemon to the poaching liquid for the additional flavour when I have them to hand, but the recipe still works well without them. Just crumble the stock cube into the water and proceed as above.

2 The yoghurt sauce is super adaptable. If horseradish isn't your thing, try the same quantity of tahini for an interesting variation, or stir a little of Yumi's pesto (page 210) into the yoghurt instead (and maybe top the salmon with basil leaves and toasted pine nuts while you're at it). Alternatively, replace the horseradish with Cheat's Tartare (page 174).

A Bowl of Mussels Two Ways

SERVES 2

1 kg (2 lb 4 oz) mussels, scrubbed and hairy beards pulled out

2 spring onions (scallions), thinly sliced

pepper, to taste

crusty bread or rice, to serve (optional)

WAY 1

75 g (2¾ oz) butter

1 garlic clove, crushed

2 fresh bay leaves

½ bunch thyme, leaves picked

½ cup (125 ml) white wine

1 large handful flat-leaf parsley leaves, finely chopped, to garnish

WAY 2

2 tablespoons vegetable oil

½ teaspoon mustard seeds

2 finely chopped red chillies

1 teaspoon turmeric powder

1 teaspoon ground cumin

1 teaspoon ground coriander

400 g (14 oz) tomatoes, roughly chopped

300 ml (10½ fl oz) coconut milk

1 tablespoon tamarind paste

1 large handful finely chopped coriander (cilantro) leaves, to garnish

A (relatively) cheap and sustainable form of seafood, mussels are also easy to cook. That's all well and good, but the fact that they taste delicious too is what really interests me. Steaming in their juices, the shells pop open, full of briny flavour and ready to take in whatever is in the pan. All you need is a spoon and some carbs for mopping and soaking.

Discard any open mussels that don't close when tapped on the bench, as well as any broken ones.

Heat the butter or oil over medium heat in a deep, non-stick saucepan that has a lid. Add the spring onion and cook for 5–6 minutes, until softened and lightly coloured.

For Way 1, add the garlic, bay leaves and thyme to the pan and cook for a further minute, or until the garlic has softened. Add the wine and bring to a simmer, then reduce the heat to low and simmer for 5–10 minutes, until thickened and reduced to your liking.

For Way 2, add the mustard seeds, chillies and spices to the pan and stir for 1–2 minutes until fragrant, then add the tomatoes and cook for 5 minutes to soften. Pour in the coconut milk, stir in the tamarind paste and bring to the boil, then reduce the heat to low and simmer for 5–10 minutes, until thickened and reduced to your liking.

Whichever path you've taken, add the mussels and a little pepper (there's no need to add salt – the mussels are salty enough), then cover and cook for 3–4 minutes, until the mussel shells open (discard any unopened mussels). Spoon the mussels and sauce into bowls, scatter over the parsley or coriander and serve as is, or with crusty bread or rice as you prefer.

When I worked as a kitchen hand, I used to have to stand at the sink elbow deep in mussels, scrubbing. Now I only ever buy them cleaned. — Yumi

TIPS

1. To make this recipe as simple as possible, buy your mussels already cleaned and debearded (from a fishmonger or the supermarket). Otherwise, clean the mussels under running water before you start, scrubbing off any dirt or seaweed and pulling out the hairy beards as necessary.

Bucket of Prawns with Spicy Sauce

SERVES 6 AS A STARTER

For a long time I was a huge believer in buying cooked prawns. You just get 'em home, upend the bag into a bowl and serve. Easy! Then, I had a midwinter revelation – I realised I just wasn't keen on that fridgey vibe. I wanted something fresher, warmer and less, well, fridge-flavoured. So I started buying raw prawns, which cost exactly the same as cooked. The cooking bit was easy. The only drawback? You have to allow them 3 whole minutes to cook!

The sauce here is entirely optional – if you prefer your prawns with lemon wedges or something else then go with it.

Combine the sauce ingredients in a bowl and give them a good stir. Set aside in the fridge until needed.

Get a large saucepan of salted water boiling and put a colander or strainer in the sink. Have a slotted spoon ready.

Cook the prawns in batches for 3 minutes. If they're particularly huge, test one after 3 minutes (by peeling and eating it) to make sure it's cooked through. Scoop the cooked prawns out of the boiling water using a slotted spoon and allow them to drain steamily in the colander. Repeat until all the prawns are cooked. (In my 'biggish' pot at home, I can do this in three batches.)

Serve the cooked prawns straight from the colander or transfer them to a fancier bowl or bucket, alongside lemon wedges and the sauce, if you made it. And don't forget you're gonna need an empty bowl for the shells and heads.

1 kg (2 lb 4 oz) medium tiger prawns (shrimp)
lemon wedges, to serve

SPICY SAUCE

1 cup (235 g) mayonnaise

1 tablespoon tomato paste (concentrated purée)

1 tablespoon sriracha

¼ teaspoon ground white pepper

I don't cook my own, but I can see why you would after this. Simple. Juicy. Great. — Simon

1. I take a freezer bag and ice brick to buy prawns so that I'm confident they're kept cool all the way home (because you never know when you might decide to make an impromptu stop and you don't want them sitting in a hot car).

2. Sometimes uncooked prawns have a sooty black discolouration around the joints. This is a naturally occurring enzyme reaction to oxygen and light and isn't bad (and in fact some chefs like it because it's proof the prawns haven't been chemically treated).

DAIRY &

DiY YOGHURT

Making yoghurt at home is nowhere near as tricky as we've been led to believe! And it's worth it because:

1.

The yoghurt itself is way better.

2.

The process involves much less single-use, virgin plastic.

3.

You'll save a bit of money.

All you need is a large thermos that can fit a 4 cup (1 litre) container (an old yoghurt container or a glass jar with a lid will work). You can buy a 'yoghurt maker', which is basically a glorified thermos, at the supermarket. Also available in supermarkets and health-food stores are sachets of culture mixture. The whole process involves tipping the powder into your container or jar, adding water, shaking it, adding a bit more water until it's full, sealing it well, then placing the container or jar in the large thermos. There's no cooking. You pour boiling water over the container or jar into the thermos, close it and leave it to set overnight. Ta-dah.

Strained yoghurt

You can go a step further by making your own strained yoghurt. Set up a straining station by placing a sieve, lined with a clean tea towel or Chux, over a bowl, and making sure this whole kit will fit in the fridge. Decant the entire 4 cups (1 litre) of chilled yoghurt into the lined sieve, gather up the sides of the tea towel or Chux, tie up with a rubber band and leave overnight in the fridge. The yoghurt will slowly release water and in the morning you will have a concentrated, 'strained' yoghurt. The whey in the bowl can be used in pancakes for a bright, sour addition.

Store in an airtight container in the fridge for up to 1 week.

Labne

To make labne, which is more of a cream cheese, mix a generous pinch of salt through the yoghurt before pouring it into the sieve as for strained yoghurt (above), and leave it in the fridge to strain for up to 48 hours.

Stored in an airtight container in the fridge for up to 1 week, or roll it into balls, coat them in za'atar spices, then store in olive oil in an airtight container in the fridge for up to 2 weeks.

Vegan Tofu Scramble

450 g (1 lb) firm tofu

¼ teaspoon turmeric powder

¼ teaspoon smoked paprika

1 tablespoon tahini

2 tablespoons nutritional yeast

½ cup (125 ml) plant-based
milk of your choice (e.g. oat,
cashew, almond)

1 tablespoon olive oil

3 spring onions (scallions),
thinly sliced

2 tomatoes, diced

salt

*This is one of my favourite
things Simon has taught me.
— Yumi*

SERVES 2

Okay, so this isn't really eggs or dairy, but much as I love eggs, it's nice to change things up a bit. This vegan scramble isn't pretending to be eggs – it has its own vibe and a bright, light feel to it – but it still delivers everything I'm looking for in the morning: crunchy toast and soft scramble.

The flavours in the tofu are based on the Colombian classic scrambled egg dish *huevos pericos* or 'parakeet eggs' (so named because of its bright colours). It's a great combination and the perfect way to push yourself outside your typical egg box.

Drain the tofu. Line a cutting board with a few layers of paper towel or a clean tea towel. Place the tofu on top, cover it with plastic wrap, put a heavy weight on it (a couple of tins of beans or a small heavy pan would do the job nicely) then leave it to sit for 15 minutes.

Meanwhile, whisk together the turmeric, paprika, tahini and nutritional yeast. Pour in the milk and whisk gradually until you have a nice sauce.

Heat the oil in a large non-stick frying pan over medium–high heat. Add the spring onions and tomatoes and cook for 2–3 minutes, then rough crumble the pressed tofu into the pan. Cook for 5–7 minutes, stirring occasionally and breaking up any large chunks of tofu as you go, until the tofu is lightly browned.

Add the sauce to the pan and stir to combine, then continue to cook until the scramble reaches your preferred texture and consistency (a 'wet' scramble will take less than 1 minute, a drier one 2–3 minutes). Season with salt and serve immediately.

1. If you're keen to give this more of an eggy flavour, try using Indian black salt (or kala namak). Available online and in good specialty stores, it has a sulfurous flavour that will deliver what you're after.

2. The tomato and spring onion combination here works well in ordinary scrambled eggs too – just cook them for a few minutes in oil or butter before adding the eggs as you normally would. Again, non-vegan, but a little crumbled feta cheese makes a delicious addition.

GF Chocolate Pancakes

2 eggs, at room temperature

⅓ cup (75 g) caster (superfine) sugar

2 teaspoons vanilla essence

½ teaspoon salt

⅓ cup (80 ml) grapeseed oil

1½ cups (375 ml) dairy-free milk of your choice

2 cups (300 g) gluten-free self-raising flour

¼ cup (30 g) good-quality unsweetened cocoa powder

1 cup (170 g) dairy-free chocolate chips

cooking oil spray

whipped cream (optional), blueberries, sliced banana and maple syrup, to serve

This recipe is fantastic. Some days I wake up and want chocolate, so a chocolate pancake recipe is just what Dr Yumi ordered. But for an excellent non-choc pancake, leave out the cocoa and choc chips.

To make the starter meringue you'll need an electric mixer, but you can completely bypass the whipping stage and the pancakes will still work out okay, just less fluffy. If you don't require a gluten-free recipe, this one works just fine with regular self-raising flour. Having tried all the milks, I'd recommend any of soy, lactose-free, regular or oat milk. All work.

Separate the eggs, putting the whites directly into the bowl of your electric mixer. Using the whisk attachment, beat the whites to soft peaks at medium speed, then gradually add the sugar to make a fluffy, glossy meringue mixture. This should take about 5 minutes from beginning to end. Add the vanilla, salt and oil, mixing at low speed until combined. Using a large metal spoon, gently fold in the milk, then finally sift in the flour and cocoa powder and fold in until just combined, aiming to keep the mixture as airy as possible. Sprinkle the choc chips over the mix once the flour is in and give the batter only a perfunctory stir.

(If you don't want to beat the egg whites first, it still works if you mix together the eggs, sugar, vanilla, salt and oil, then add the milk, mix again, and finally sift in the flour and cocoa powder and stir gently until just combined. Sprinkle over the choc chips once the flour is in and give the batter a quick stir.)

Preheat a medium–large frying pan over medium–high heat, spray it well with cooking oil spray then reduce the heat to medium. Pour in ½ cup (125 ml) batter for each pancake. (The average frying pan will comfortably fit three pancakes. Don't go for more, or they will be overcrowded and difficult to handle.) Immediately cover the pan with a lid and set a timer for 3 minutes. When the time is up, remove the lid. The uncooked tops of the pancakes should be bubbled and looking ready to flip. (If not, replace the lid and give them another minute.) Flip each pancake and cook for another 2 minutes with the lid off.

Serve with fat dollops of whipped cream (if using), blueberries, sliced banana and a drizzle of maple syrup.

1. Some of the choc chips will scorch a little where they touch the frying pan. This is totally okay.

2. Obviously, if you use whipped cream, the recipe is no longer dairy-free. If you don't need dairy-free, milk chocolate chips are great here.

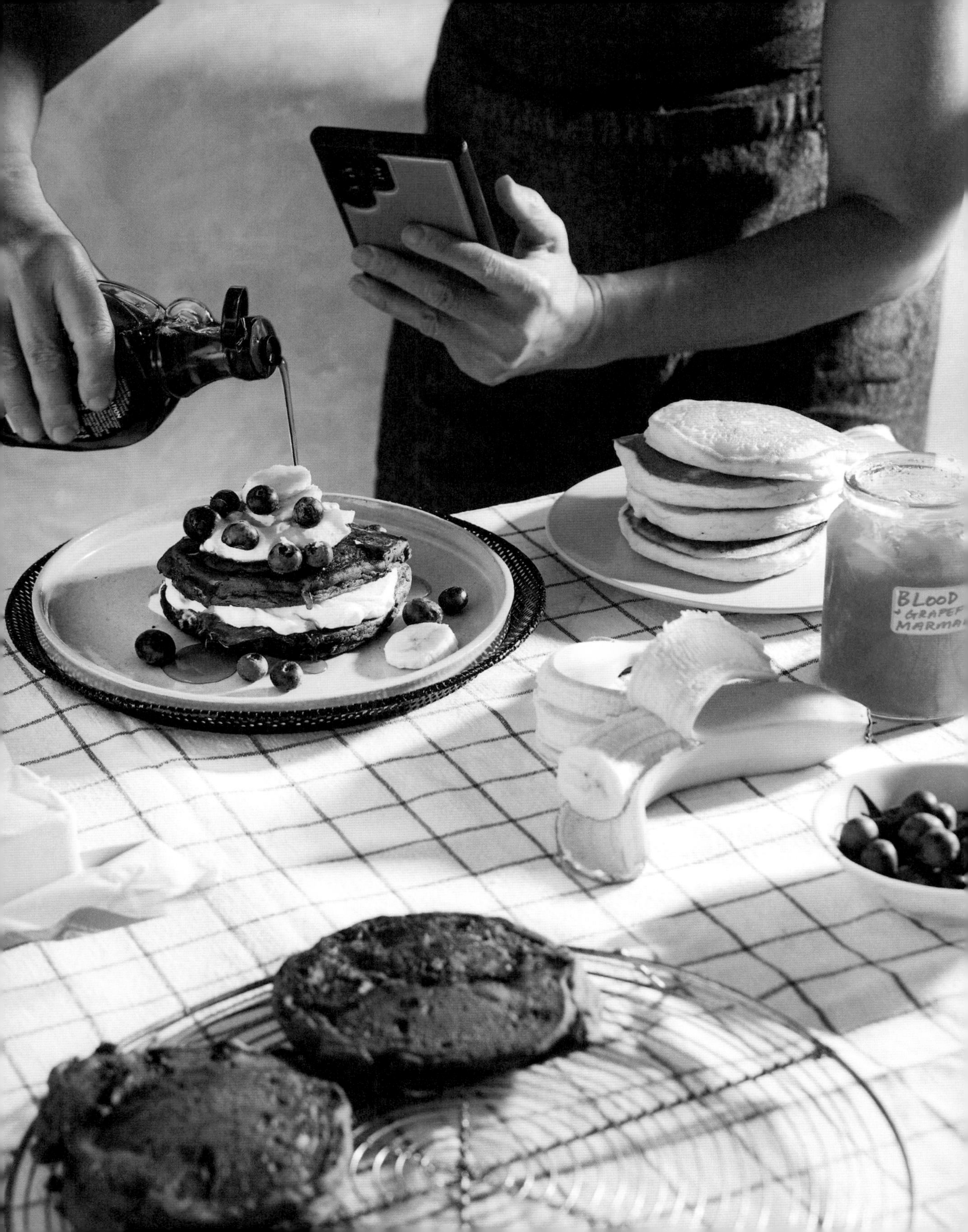
BLOOD

Creamy Bacon Penne

250 g (9 oz) penne, spiral
or rigatoni pasta

180 g (6¼ oz) bacon

150 g (5½ oz) sour cream

1 egg

40 g (1½ oz) grated Grana Padano
or parmesan cheese, plus extra
to serve

SERVES 3

This recipe is AWESOME. As a single mum cooking mostly for three (me and my two smaller ones) I try to cook just enough to have a little emergency half-serve of leftovers. If you need more, double the ingredients and use a bigger pasta pot.

Each element is simple – the only tricky thing is stirring the egg mixture through the pasta at the end without scrambling the egg. Watch closely as you go, and be prepared to pause if necessary.

Cook the pasta for 1 minute less than the packet directions.

Meanwhile, cut the bacon into matchsticks and set aside. Combine the sour cream, egg and cheese in a small bowl or jug, mixing well.

Heat a large frying pan over medium–low heat and gently fry the bacon until cooked.

When draining the pasta, reserve ½ cup (125 ml) of the pasta water (have a measuring cup sitting in the sink next to the colander).

Combine the drained pasta and fried bacon in the now-empty pasta pot. (You can also choose to go the other way and tip the pasta into the bacon pan: whatever's easiest for you and so long as it all fits.) Remove from the heat and toss to mix.

Pour the sour cream and egg mixture onto the pasta. When you're confident the pan is not too scorching, add a splash of the pasta water then mix everything through. The sauce will emulsify around the pasta pieces – this is good.

Serve immediately and top with more cheese if requested.

Because I'm a pasta snob, I'd
leave out the cream, switch the
bacon for pancetta/guanciale
and call this a carbonara. But
then the kids wouldn't eat it.
So, who's the real winner?
— Simon

1. This is good with A Side of Burnished Broccoli (page 77).
2. If you want your kids to eat more protein, you can add a second egg to this recipe.

GET YOUR PASTA RIGHT

Pasta – for something so simple, so many things can go wrong. Follow the guidelines below and your pasta game will never be less than perfect.

* Always use your largest pan for boiling pasta water – the more space the pasta has to move around while cooking, the better.

* Be sure to salt the pasta water heavily (you want it as salty as the sea, so about 2 teaspoons/10 g per litre). As the pasta cooks, this salt seasons it from the inside out all the way through, meaning you'll need to add less at the end and the noodles will be far tastier.

* Cook your pasta only until it's 'al dente' (that's Italian for 'to the tooth'), which simply means checking it every few minutes until you have something that still has a little bite to it in the centre. Don't trust the packet directions on this – they tend to be a bit conservative. As a rough rule of thumb, subtract a minute or two from the recommended time and you'll be right.

* Hard to judge how much pasta per person? Weigh it until you feel comfortable guessing by eye – around 80–100 g (2¾–3½ oz) of dried pasta per person is a standard adult portion, depending on whether you're talking starter or main.

* Choose the right pasta for the right sauce. You could go down the rabbit hole on this (google it and see for yourself) but generally speaking, something creamy, smooth and unctuous calls for long noodles such as spaghetti or tagliatelle, while a chunky, rough sauce calls for something short like penne, rigatoni or farfalle with holes or folds for catching all that goodness.

* Be sure to mix your sauce through your pasta before serving. (Don't plonk it on top like a comedy hat – that's a sure-fire way to dry, claggy noodles and sad times.) Reserve a cup of the pasta cooking water before draining, then add it back to the pan with the pasta and sauce little by little, until everything is combined and the texture is luscious and silky.

* Never, never, never use quick-cook pasta. Its texture is horrible and none of us is so busy that we can't wait that extra couple of minutes.

* Don't break your spaghetti in half before cooking. Please. It's long for a reason – it tastes better this way.

* Finish your pasta with Grana Padano or parmesan cheese, if you like, but try to avoid the stuff that comes grated in bags, which often tastes like cardboard shavings compared to the real thing.

Shakshuka

SERVES 2–4

For me, this is the ultimate egg dish. I find the way the yolks ooze into that rich spiced, onion-laced and herb-flecked sauce endlessly appealing. All you need are some toasted flatbreads for scooping and you're away.

First things first, make sure the sauce has reduced properly before adding the eggs. Second, keep your eye on the eggs to ensure that the heat from the bubbling sauce underneath has turned all the translucent white opaque before you remove the pan from the heat. I like to spoon the eggs into bowls just at this point, then cover them with the sauce to let its residual heat cook the yolks through, before pulling them apart, but you might want to cook them a little longer.

Heat the olive oil in a large frying pan over medium heat. Add the onion, smoked paprika and coriander seeds, if using, and cook for 10 minutes, stirring occasionally, until the onions are lightly golden. Add the garlic and chilli, if using, and cook, stirring, for a further minute.

Tip in the chopped tomatoes, bring to a vigorous simmer and cook away, stirring, for 10–15 minutes until thick, jammy and delicious. Season with salt and pepper to taste.

Stir in the peas and parsley until mixed evenly, then use the back of a wooden spoon to make little 'craters' or indents in the sauce. Reduce the heat to low, then crack the eggs into the craters (1–2 per person) and simmer gently for 3–4 minutes, or until the eggs are looking just cooked through (pop a lid on top if you're a little worried about this).

Serve with toasted flatbreads, and either divide the shakshuka between serving bowls or set the pan on a heatproof mat in the middle of the table in flashy style like the culinary rockstar you have become.

Too farty for me. — Yumi

1 tablespoon olive oil

1 onion, thinly sliced

2 teaspoons smoked paprika

1 teaspoon coriander seeds, crushed (optional)

1 garlic clove, finely chopped

1 fresh red chilli, finely chopped (optional)

800 g (1 lb 12 oz) tinned chopped tomatoes

salt and pepper

¾ cup (100 g) frozen baby peas

2 large handfuls flat-leaf parsley or coriander (cilantro), roughly chopped, plus extra to serve

4–8 eggs

toasted flatbreads, to serve

1. The spices I've used here are pretty arbitrary. If coriander seeds aren't for you, then leave them out (maybe try cumin). Likewise, the chilli adds a lovely fruitiness along with a blast of heat – but if you're not keen the sauce will still taste great without it.

2. I've popped peas in here but lots of other vegetables work really well in this sauce, too. Try sautéing some red capsicum strips or zucchini (courgette) slices with the onion, or adding bite-sized chunks of roasted veg such as pumpkin (squash) – or even a handful or two of baby spinach leaves – at the point when you add the peas.

3. For different (but no less delicious) results, use an ovenproof pan, grate some parmesan cheese over or crumble in some feta cheese and flash-cook it under a hot grill just after the point when you add the eggs.

Stuffed Pasta Shells

SERVES 2–3

People are coming over. You have to feed them. Are you going to stand there stressing, wearing an oven mitt and a frown of doom, unable to hear anything anyone is saying? No! You're going to do something yummy and easy that won't require any of your attention when your friends arrive.

Here, tomato passata is the entire sauce – no reducing, no onion-chopping. It's pretty easy to throw together, to be forgotten until required. Either make ahead and store it in the fridge until it's time to get baking, or have it in the oven when people arrive.

As with the bacon penne recipe on page 144, I make this to serve my little family of three. If you're feeding more, double the quantities and use two baking dishes.

Bring a large saucepan or pasta pot of well-salted water to the boil and preheat the oven to 180°C (350°F).

Cook the pasta for about half of the time recommended in the packet directions.

Meanwhile, grease your chosen baking dish with butter.

Combine half the Grana Padano cheese with the ricotta cheese and egg, and mix well. The mixture should be cheesy and creamy. If making the luxe version, add the extra ingredients now.

When the pasta is cooked, drain well. Pour half of the tomato passata into the baking dish. Fill one pasta shell at a time with the cheesy mixture. It might be easier to scrape the filling into the pasta shell by dragging it along the side of the mixing bowl. Either that or use a teaspoon. Cram all the filled shells into the baking dish, then top with the remaining tomato passata and scatter the remaining Grana Padano cheese over.

Bake for 20 minutes, then switch the oven to the hot grill setting and cook the top of the dish for another 5 minutes.

I like to serve this dish with a garnish of fresh basil leaves and lots of crusty bread to dip into that molten red, cheesy sauce.

Switch the passata for my Emergency Tomato Pasta Sauce #1 (page 22) for an EVEN more excellent version here. — Simon

UTTERLY BASIC VERSION

150 g (5½ oz) large shell pasta (conchiglioni rigati)

butter, for greasing

100 g (3½ oz) Grana Padano cheese

350 g (12 oz) ricotta cheese

1 large egg

2 cups (500 ml) tomato passata (puréed tomatoes)

EXTRAS FOR THE MOST EXCELLENT VERSION

1 cup (45 g) baby spinach, very finely chopped

2–3 whispers of freshly grated nutmeg

pepper, to taste

1. To figure out how much pasta to cook and which baking dish to use, tip the uncooked pasta into the baking dish. You should be able to spread the pieces out so they're not overlapping but fit tightly in one layer with not too many gaps. Scale up the recipe depending on how many you're feeding.

2. If you have left-over pumpkin (from page 97, for example), you can replace the ricotta with skinless cooked pumpkin for very delicious results.

3. I often serve this with a jar of sambal oelek on the table so anyone who wants some chilli spice can help themselves. If everyone likes chilli, then before cooking, mix 2 tablespoons sambal oelek through the tomato passata.

Crispy Paneer and Watermelon Salad

SERVES 4–6

Since we moved to Australia, summer has meant melon on high rotation in our house, and it often works its way into refreshing salads like this. While this sort of watermelon salad is often made with feta, I like the contrast of texture and nutty, toasted flavour that the crispy paneer brings to the party here. And yes, haloumi works well too, but be aware that it will become chewier rather than crisp when fried. Not necessarily a bad thing – just different.

Coarsely grate the paneer.

Heat the oil in a large frying pan over medium heat. Add the paneer and fry, stirring, for 3–4 minutes, until a lovely orangey gold all over. Transfer to paper towel to drain (it will crisp up further as it cools).

Scoop out the watermelon flesh and chop it into chunks, discarding the rind and pips. Thinly slice the onion, then pick the mint and coriander leaves, tearing any larger ones. Squeeze the olives between thumb and forefinger to press out the pits, then tear the flesh into small pieces.

Combine everything in a bowl and toss. Drizzle over a little oil and season with pepper.

200 g (7 oz) paneer cheese

1 tablespoon extra virgin olive oil, plus extra for drizzling

700 g (1 lb 9 oz) watermelon

1 small red onion

1 bunch fresh mint

1 bunch fresh coriander (cilantro)

20 semi-dried kalamata olives or regular kalamata olives

pepper, to taste

Paneer is awesome! And getting easier to find. You'll get the best deal at an Indian grocer. — Yumi

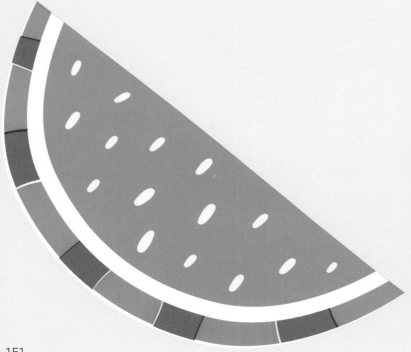

TiPS

1. For a little extra jolt of flavour, try replacing the red onion with Quick-pickled Red Onion slices (page 214).

2. If you don't like coriander, feel free to replace it with flat-leaf parsley or double the quantity of mint instead.

3. While the semi-dried kalamata olives are a bit harder to find, it's worth hunting them down if you can – they're not stored in brine or liquid, keep for ages in the fridge and are perfect for salads like this and for scattering over pizzas or adding to braises and casseroles.

4. We're now veering into very unusual territory here, but Yumi's Wedding-guest Croutons (page 204) work a treat scattered over the top. If you're struggling with that mental image, maybe try to think of it as a watermelon panzanella?

Ricotta Gnocchi

I freakin' love gnocchi, and home-made gnocchi is always better than store-bought. But I'm such a devotee of zero-fucks cooking that I've had to work hard to reconcile the idea of making gnocchi from scratch with my absolute refusal to do more work than necessary in the kitchen. This recipe is the result, and it's quick, and the quicker you make it, the better the results, so treat the whole damn thing like a race, where first prize is puffy, fat dumplings of deliciousness. Uncooked gnocchi freeze well so you can stash plenty away for later.

Drain any watery liquid off the ricotta so that it's as dry as possible. Combine all ingredients except the flour in a large bowl and mix well.

Clear a good amount of clean bench space and make sure the flour is close to hand. Bring a large saucepan of well-salted water to the boil.

Add 200 g (7 oz) flour to the ricotta mixture and combine. Mix it with your hands, feeling for whether it could be rolled and hold its shape. You want to perform minimal mixing while using minimal extra flour. If you're unsure, plop a sample ball into the boiling water and see if it holds its shape – wait until the gnocchi floats, then try it. (It may withstand the boiling but not, say, being skewered by a fork.)

When the dough feels right, cut it into four, then roll each quarter into a long sausage. Cut into gnocchi-sized pieces. Allow 100 g (3½ oz) gnocchi per person. Lay any remaining uncooked gnocchi on a baking tray and pop in the freezer. Once frozen, transfer to airtight containers or snaplock bags and freeze for up to 3 months (they can be cooked from frozen).

Drop the gnocchi into the boiling water: they will float when cooked (2–3 minutes). Stand by with a slotted spoon ready to scoop them out.

Because the gnocchi are so good, they don't need much more than a simple sauce. The following are all designed to feed 1 (when you're home alone, this is self-care).

Butter and sage: Fry a handful of sage leaves in 3–4 tablespoons butter. Once the leaves are crispy, toss the hot gnocchi through and season.

Truffle: Toss 2 tablespoons cold truffle butter through the hot gnocchi.

Pesto: Loosen 2 tablespoons pesto (homemade on page 210, or store-bought) with a few spoonfuls of cooking water, add lots of pepper, then toss the gnocchi through and serve with extra cheese (pictured opposite).

Blue cheese: Toast 1 tablespoon pine nuts In a dry frying pan over low heat. When golden, add 50 g (1¾ oz) blue cheese, 2 tablespoons sour cream and black pepper. Stir until melted together. When it's sauce-like, toss the hot gnocchi through, and prepare to die of pleasure.

500 g (1 lb 2 oz) fresh ricotta cheese

150 g (5½ oz) finely grated Grana Padano cheese

2 eggs

1 egg yolk

1 teaspoon salt

pepper, to taste

2–3 whispers of freshly grated nutmeg

250–300 g strong ('00') flour

1 For this you need to use the ricotta cheese sold in baskets at the deli counter. It won't work with the stuff that comes in a plastic container.

2 Just before cooking, you can roll the gnocchi on a fork or a gnocchi board to get those distinctive ridges (I don't always bother).

Chawanmushi

2 large eggs

350 ml (12 fl oz) dashi

1 teaspoon mirin (sweet rice wine)

1 teaspoon soy sauce (light-coloured usukuchi soy sauce if possible)

4 peeled prawn tails

8 shelled edamame beans

4 sugarsnap peas, trimmed

1 tablespoon finely chopped spring onion (scallion)

10 g (¼ oz) shimeji or other mushrooms (shiitake left over from page 114 are perfect)

4 small soft green herb sprigs (e.g. coriander/cilantro, parsley, Japanese parsley, inner celery leaves)

4 slices Japanese fish cake (available from Asian grocers in the freezer)

Chawanmushi , a Japanese savoury custard, is an incredibly unctuous and nourishing way to start a meal. My mum used to make it in my childhood and I always order it when I'm in Japan. I thought you had to be a master to make it – until I actually tried and realised it's very straightforward. The trick is to strain the egg so there are no stringy bits, and to cook very gently to avoid creating bubbles. The recipe is quite adaptable to customisation, but start here before making any improvisations. You'll need serving cups such as 1 cup (250 ml) ramekins, large green tea cups or chawanmushi cups that will fit inside a large saucepan with its lid on.

Organise a large saucepan with your chosen serving cups inside it, making sure the lid fits snugly. Make sure your saucepan isn't so deep that it's hard to get the cups in and out. Pour water into the saucepan so that it comes halfway up the sides of the cups. Now you know exactly how much water you need, you can take out the cups and start the recipe.

Whisk the eggs then gently add the dashi, mirin and soy sauce, taking care to avoid creating bubbles and/or froth.

In the bottom of each cup, place 1 prawn, 2 edamame beans, a sugarsnap pea and 1 teaspoon spring onion. Trim the shimeji mushroom of any tough stem, divide into four and add that next. Pour the egg mixture into each cup through a tea strainer. You should have about 110 g (3¾ oz) per cup. Top each cup with a pinch of green herb and a slice of fish cake.

If the cups don't have lids, cover each one with a square of foil. (They can be successfully steamed without foil, but steamy condensation will drip back into the cups and leave holes in the custard.)

Bring the water in the saucepan to a very gentle boil, then carefully lower the cups into the saucepan, cover with the lid and steam over low heat with the water very lightly simmering for 15 minutes. You don't want the cups rattling around in there, just the most gentle steam. Check whether the custard is set by removing the lid or foil from one of the cups and tilting it carefully. Serve warm with a small spoon.

A note on dashi

Dashi is a stock made from bonito fish flakes and kombu seaweed concentrate. It can be bought in concentrated bottled form, or in a powder, or you can make it yourself by soaking kombu and bonito overnight then cooking and straining. Most convenient is the powdered version, which is easy to find, and can be reconstituted by mixing one 5 g (⅛ oz) sachet with 350 ml (12 fl oz) water, which turns out to be the precise amount required for this recipe.

1. These can also be cooked inside a steaming basket, but my steamer isn't tall enough to take my cups.

2. I have tried all the different dashi stocks in this, including homemade, and it makes so little difference that I'd just go for the easiest option.

3. If you become a superfan, you can buy wonderfully ornate, lidded chawanmushi cups from specialty Japanese cookware shops.

Pork in Milk

1 lemon

2 kg (4 lb 8 oz) boned loin of pork, rind and fat removed

salt and pepper

2 tablespoons extra virgin olive oil

50 g (1¾ oz) butter

10 garlic cloves, peeled

1 small handful sage leaves or 1 small rosemary sprig (optional)

about 6 cups (1.5 litres) whole milk

Yes, this might not sound particularly appealing, but trust me, it's worth making. A classic Tuscan one-pot wonder and a stalwart in the early days of London's iconic Italian restaurant the River Café, it's since been pushed around the world in various guises by probably its most famous alumnus, a certain Jamie Oliver. There's a reason for this – cooking the meat in the milk gives melt-in-the-mouth results and incredible flavour in return for exceedingly little effort on behalf of the cook. Serve it with mashed potato or creamy polenta, or alongside Yumi's Harissa Pumpkin (page 97) with some squeaky green beans, then watch the compliments roll in.

Using a vegetable peeler, peel the rind off the lemon in big, swirling pieces. Set aside. Generously season the trimmed pork with salt and pepper all over.

Heat the olive oil over medium heat in a large heavy-bottomed saucepan with a lid or a cast-iron casserole dish large enough to hold the pork. Brown the meat all over, then remove from the pan.

Drain any excess fat from the pan, then add the butter. Once the butter has melted, add the garlic and sage or rosemary, if using, and cook until the garlic begins to colour. Return the pork to the pan and add enough milk to come three-quarters of the way up the sides of the meat. Bring to the boil and add the lemon rind, then reduce the heat to low and cover with the lid, leaving it slightly askew. Simmer slowly for 1½–2 hours, resisting the temptation to disturb the meat as it cooks, until the milk has curdled into brown nuggets.

Remove from the heat and leave to sit for 10 minutes, then carefully remove the meat from the pan and cut into thin slices. Serve immediately with the sauce spooned over it.

1. Don't be worried by those milky nuggets that form in the pan; these are the result of the milk separating as the pork is braised in it. While not particularly pretty, they deliver full-on flavour and are all part of the science of this dish – it's the lactic acid in the milk that helps transform the meat into something so fall-apart and flavoursome. If you're put off by the nuggets, you can always whiz them up in a blender at the end with a little cream, if you like, for a smoother, more aesthetically pleasing alternative.

2. Any left-over meat here would be great shredded and stirred through pasta with spinach, toasted pine nuts and a dollop or two of crème fraîche thinned out with a little of the pasta cooking water.

RESTAURANT FOOD iS NOT HOME FOOD

(OR WHY MASTERCHEF DOESN'T MEAN MASTER COOK)

If there's one thing you should take from the legions of competitive cooking shows doing the rounds on TV these days it's that cooking at home is nothing like that.

Yup, in the same way that porn and actual, real-life sex between consenting adults are not at all the same thing, the food that's presented on a competitive cooking show is so far removed from what gets served up for dinner at home that we may as well class them as entirely separate entities. It's not even apples and oranges. More apples and that weird spray 'cheese' you can get in the supermarket that would probably work better for shaving than eating.

I'm not saying you shouldn't enjoy these shows, just be aware that what's offered up to the judges to taste isn't some gold standard of cooking at all but a highly dramatised, overwrought version of restaurant food that often lives or dies on how OTT it is or how compelling the competitor's 'journey' up to this point has been. This isn't how food or cooking should be at home. Ever. And nor should it be!

Also remember that restaurants and culinary professionals can do lots of things you can't. They have blowtorches, sous vide machines, blast chillers and whole battalions of people working to get those elements of a dish on a plate right and looking stupendous. (The food,

also, as a rule, relies on numerous sneaky tricks to make it taste delicious, including an inordinate amount of butter and salt – fine for a treat, less good for the arteries when eaten every day.) Home cooking, on the other hand, plays best in a completely different part of the culinary pool, and for very good reasons.

How does this translate to the average home cook? Well, think of the foods that a home cook can do well that a restaurant just can't. Concentrate on big communal dishes that embrace sharing, like oven bakes and roasts: any foods that aren't geared towards the individual. You want dishes where timing isn't super critical to success (ever tried cooking individual steaks for ten? Not so easy) and where plating-up doesn't involve drawing a sketch beforehand or building towers or spheres or including things like 'soils' (urgh!).

Now don't get me wrong. I utterly adore restaurants and restaurant food (I mean, honestly, who doesn't love it when someone else does the cooking and washing up for you, lets you choose what you want to eat, and hopefully also makes it both look fancy and taste incredible?). But once you accept that certain things are best left in a restaurant setting and that great home cooking should be something different entirely, I promise you your life in the kitchen will become infinitely more enjoyable.

FREEZ

FORK

Green Pea Guacamole

When this guacamole was busy setting the New York food world alight a few years back, strong opinions were formed, with then-president Barack Obama himself even weighing in on the subject (he came down in favour of no peas, fyi). Now, far be it from me to argue with the former leader of the free world, but in this instance I think he's wrong. Frozen peas add a delightful grassy-green freshness and a lovely textural pop to the creamy avocado. Yes, it's also a clever way to pad out all that potentially expensive fruit, but I'll be *coughs* barracking for peas in guac for life from now on.

Blanch the peas by plunging them in a saucepan of boiling salted water for 1 minute, then draining and running under the cold tap until cool.

Tip half the peas into a bowl and mash with a fork. Scoop the avocado flesh into the bowl together with the garlic, chilli, coriander and lime juice, then mash together until the guac has your preferred consistency (I like mine a little chunky, but if you prefer things super smooth, go for it). Add the remaining peas and olive oil and mix together gently, then season to taste with salt and pepper, adding a little extra squeeze of lime juice if you need it to get the whole thing to zing.

1 cup (140 g) frozen peas

2 avocados

1 small garlic clove, finely grated

1 fresh green chilli, finely chopped

1–2 large handfuls coriander (cilantro) leaves, finely chopped

juice of 1–2 limes, plus extra as needed

1 tablespoon extra virgin olive oil

salt and pepper

People think you're way more clever than you are when you serve this. — Yumi

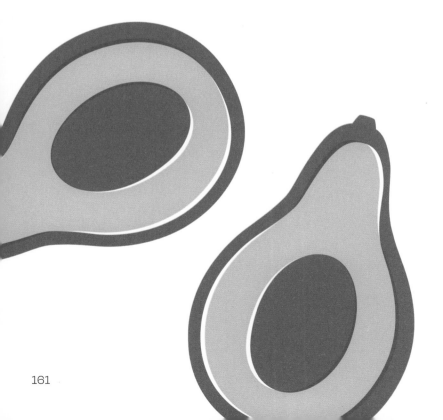

TiPS

1. Do increase or reduce the ratio of peas to avocado here to suit your own personal preference or take into account costs in the shops.

2. And in case you thought I couldn't defile guacamole any further, this is also really good with the same amount of sweetcorn instead of the peas, either tinned and drained or grilled and chopped off the cob. You could even add a nice big crumble of feta cheese while you're at it.

Pea and Pesto Soup

2 tablespoons butter

1 onion, finely chopped

3 cups (750 ml) chicken
   or vegetable stock

500 g (1 lb 2 oz) frozen baby peas

1 teaspoon salt

½ teaspoon pepper

3 tablespoons Yumi's Perfect Pesto
   (page 210)

Greek-style yoghurt or crème fraîche,
   to serve

olive oil, for drizzling

Wedding-guest Croutons (page 204),
   to serve

SERVES 4–6

I don't really get giddy with excitement at the thought of soup. But whenever I do get around to it, I'm always surprised by how much I love it. There's definitely a time and a place for a bowl of the good stuff, and for me that's a quiet lunch of a quick soup made with ingredients I have easily to hand, with something swirled through it to liven things up, a dollop of cold yoghurt to set things off, a generous scattering of crispy croutons for crunch and texture, and hunks of bread for mopping and dipping. This one fits the bill nicely.

Heat the butter in a large saucepan, add the onion and cook over medium–low heat for 5–10 minutes, until the onion is soft. Add the stock and bring to a boil. Add the peas and cook for 3 minutes, until tender. Remove from the heat and add the salt and pepper.

To purée the soup in batches, place 1 cup (250 ml) soup in a blender, place the lid on top, and purée on low speed. With the blender still running, open the venthole in the lid and slowly add more soup until the blender is three-quarters full. Pour the soup into a large bowl and repeat until all the soup is puréed (or use a hand-held blender and purée the soup in the pan in one go).

Stir through the pesto, then taste and adjust the seasoning. Serve hot with dollops of Greek-style yoghurt, a drizzle of olive oil and a hefty scattering of croutons.

TIPS

1 I like to use chicken stock (ideally one I've made using left-over roast chicken; see page 106) but veg stock is good too; and stock/bouillon powder, stock in a carton or stock cubes will all do the job. Just use what you have to hand and don't get hung up on it.

2 If you haven't made up the pesto, a fresh store-bought tub would work nicely. Alternatively, add 1 handful chopped mint or basil leaves. You can also use store-bought croutons, but give Yumi's a go if you can – they're amazing!

Risi e Bisi

4 cups (1 litre) vegetable or chicken stock (page 103)

2 tablespoons extra virgin olive oil

2 garlic cloves, finely chopped

1 onion, finely chopped

1 cup (250 ml) risotto rice

½ cup (125 ml) white wine

1½ cups (195 g) frozen baby peas

a knob of butter

juice of 1 lemon

1 handful flat-leaf parsley leaves, finely chopped (optional)

salt and pepper

finely grated parmesan or Grana Padano cheese, to serve

This soupy risotto is a Venetian speciality traditionally made with fresh peas and presented to the doge on feast day. But that's not why I've included it in this book. It's here because a) now that I've replaced fresh peas with frozen it's made up of ingredients I always have to hand, and b) it's seriously easy to make, as there's no slow adding of stock to rice and patient stirring, ladleful by ladleful. You just pour in all the broth in one go, put on a lid and let it simmer away. And the whole family loves it too, which always helps.

Bring the stock to the boil in a small saucepan over medium heat, then reduce the heat to low and keep at a gentle simmer.

Meanwhile, heat the oil in a separate large saucepan over medium–low heat. Add the garlic and onion, and cook, stirring frequently, for 4 minutes or until softened. Add the rice and stir for 1 minute to coat the grains in oil, then pour in the wine and stir for 1 minute or until completely absorbed.

Add the hot stock and half the peas and bring to a simmer, then reduce the heat to low and cook, covered, for about 20 minutes, or until the rice is al dente.

Stir through the remaining peas, butter, lemon juice and parsley, if using, and season to taste with salt and pepper. Serve with parmesan or Grana Padano scattered on top.

Simon pronounces this 'rizzi bizzi' which is apparently legit but also hilarious. — Yumi

 TiPS

1   Ignore the risotto purists – any risotto rice will work absolutely fine here (and in all risotto recipes, actually). In fact, at a push any short-grain rice would still be delicious. (I once had a notable success with paella rice when scrabbling through the cupboards and finding them otherwise bare.)

2   While we're breaking with tradition, a crumble of feta at the end and a drizzle of balsamic vinegar over the top before serving work wonders, too.

THE PRINCIPLES OF TEMPERATURE

On the cooktop

It's frustrating to see a lot of beginner cooks cooking the absolute shit out of their pots and pans by having the flame too high. There's NO situation where it's appropriate for the flame to be wider than the base of the pot. It's a waste of energy, it can burn your food and it in no way hastens the cooking process. You also end up cooking the handle of the pan which can stink and release toxins if it's plastic. Check in on the relationship between the level of heat and the bottom of your pan multiple times while cooking. (Also, don't light cigarettes off the flame on the hob if you like your eyelashes.)

In the oven

Every oven is different, but you get to use yours over and over again, so you'll learn how it works, if it has hot spots and if it takes ages to warm up. If you're stuck with a really dicey oven, you can buy an oven thermometer for about $12. It won't fix your oven, but at least you'll know what temperature it's at.

A key consideration before you even turn the oven on is which shelf to use. Most ovens are hotter at the top, so if you want your food to brown, set the shelf closer to the top. But if you want a blasted bottom for, say, a pizza crust, then down low is better. If you have just one dish to bake, the middle shelf is usually best. Once you start adding multiple dishes on multiple shelves, you may need to rotate them from shelf to shelf so they cook evenly. Bear in mind, though, that you want to open the door (which releases the heat) as little as possible.

Try to remember to arrange the shelves in the right places before you start warming up the oven. Make sure the large chicken will fit before you try shoving it in the hot oven. If anything needs preheating – oil in a tray for roast potatoes (page 50) or trays for pizza bases (page 44) – then get them in while the oven is warming up.

On your plate

Some foods aren't necessarily the best right after they come off the heat. A steak or a roast chicken needs to rest and cool a little for its flavours to really speak. And many foods aren't at their best when they're fridge-cold – cheese, salad or even a simple sandwich isn't going to be interesting, nuanced or all that enjoyable if eaten straight out of the fridge. Warm to room-temperature food allows you to taste the flavours. And as a bonus your plate won't be sweating (too cold) and the roof of your mouth won't get a third-degree burn (too hot).

Keeping things warm

Restaurants place their food under heat lamps and warm plates and bowls to account for the fact that their food might be sitting for a few minutes before waitstaff can whisk it to a table. You won't have heat lamps at home, but for meals you want to serve warm, such as soup, pasta, a stir-fry or a big roast, you can warm up the plates, particularly in cold weather. The quickest and easiest way I've found to make a bowl or plate hot is to pour boiling water directly onto it while it sits in the sink. When you're ready for it, carefully tip off the water, give it a quick dry with a clean tea towel, and plate that meal.

Tomato Tarts

SERVES 4–6

Based on a classic by legendary English cook Delia Smith, these super-simple tomato tarts are my go-to in the summer months because they give maximum payback for incredibly little effort. The tomato, thyme and feta work their magic in the oven to create a delicate but incredibly flavoursome tart that you'll want to make and eat on repeat.

I suggest keeping a pack of frozen puff pastry sheets in the freezer at all times. They can step in and do the heavy lifting when you want to turn out something impressive without any of the messing around. That's a win in my book.

Preheat the oven to 190°C (375°F). Line two large baking trays with baking paper and place a sheet of pastry on each tray.

Put the feta in a small bowl and add half the olive oil with the garlic, thyme and a good seasoning of pepper. Mix everything together with a fork to make a paste.

Using a sharp knife, carefully score a line on each pastry sheet about 1 cm (½ inch) from the edge, all the way around, being careful not to cut all the way through. Using the back of a spoon, carefully spread the cheese mixture over the pastry, right up to the line.

Thinly slice the tomatoes and arrange them on top of the cheese mixture in overlapping lines. Season with salt and pepper then drizzle the remaining olive oil over and scatter over a few extra thyme sprigs.

Bake on the middle shelf of the oven for 55 minutes, or until the pastry is golden brown and the tomatoes are roasted and slightly charred at the edges. Remove from the oven and leave for 10 minutes before cutting into squares. Serve sprinkled with salt flakes and a drizzle of extra virgin olive oil.

2 sheets (about 20 g/¾ oz) frozen puff pastry, just thawed

150 g (5½ oz) Danish-style feta cheese

2 tablespoons extra virgin olive oil, plus extra for drizzling

2 garlic cloves, crushed

3 teaspoons chopped thyme leaves, plus extra to decorate

salt and pepper

725 g (1 lb 9½ oz) ripe tomatoes

1. The thyme gives a lovely warm flavour to the tomatoes but could be replaced with rosemary or oregano (perhaps just use a little less). Likewise, the feta can be replaced with a soft goat's cheese.

2. These tarts are great for a barbecue or outdoor summer lunch, and work well served cold at a picnic – just be careful to slice them and wrap them up with plastic wrap well before transporting them, as they are quite delicate.

Filo Fish Pie

SERVES 4

Some foods just scream comfort; they're the ones we turn to when we need the culinary equivalent of that big, warm cashmere jumper. Fish pie is one of these cosseting classics, but the time it takes to make a traditional one means that was very rarely an option in our house, until I discovered this method. Using hot-smoked fish, a yoghurt and milk mix instead of white sauce and store-bought filo pastry rather than the traditional mashed potato results in something different but still essentially the same. A cardigan instead of a jumper, perhaps, but no less warm or snuggly.

Preheat the oven to 180°C (350°F).

Combine the milk, eggs, parsley or dill, yoghurt, mustard and paprika, if using, in a bowl and mix well.

In a separate large bowl, combine the prawns, trout or salmon, peas and fennel, then spoon into an 8 cup (2 litre) baking dish. Pour the milk mixture over the top.

Brush one side of each filo sheet all over with the melted butter and place them in a pile. Gently scrunch up the pastry and lay it on top of the pie filling to cover it completely. Bake for 25–30 minutes in the middle of the oven until the pastry is golden and crisp. Leave to cool slightly, then serve with the lemon wedges. A nice green salad or some of Yumi's Burnished Broccoli (page 77) would go well with this, too.

Making fish pie has always scared me ... it seems high stakes. But this one works! — Yumi

1 cup (250 ml) milk

2 eggs, lightly beaten

1 small handful flat-leaf parsley leaves or dill, roughly chopped

½ cup (130 g) Greek-style yoghurt

2 teaspoons Dijon mustard

1 teaspoon smoked paprika (optional)

20 large raw prawns (shrimp), peeled and deveined

1 whole hot-smoked rainbow trout or 2 x 150 g (5½ oz) hot-smoked trout or salmon fillets, flaked

1 cup (140 g) frozen peas, thawed

1 small fennel bulb, very finely chopped

8 sheets (about 165 g) filo pastry

100 g (3½ oz) unsalted butter, melted and cooled slightly

lemon wedges, to serve

1 I like the subtle flavour of fennel here, but if you're not keen, you can always use other veg instead – zucchini (courgette) or baby spinach leaves (or a combination of the two) will also work nicely.

2 I'm afraid I can never be bothered with individual pie dishes (partly for selfish reasons, as it limits me to eating only a quarter), but if you're keen on them divide the filling and pastry between four 350 ml (12 oz) individual pie dishes instead.

Prawn Oven-tray Curry

200 g (7 oz) cherry tomatoes

1 red capsicum (pepper), thinly sliced

1 onion, roughly sliced

1 thumb-sized piece (about 5 cm/ 2 inches) fresh ginger, grated

2 teaspoons mustard seeds or nigella seeds

1 teaspoon pepper

1 teaspoon ground coriander

2 teaspoons ground cumin

1 teaspoon garam masala

1 handful fresh curry leaves (optional)

1 teaspoon salt, plus extra to taste

1 tablespoon sunflower or vegetable oil

400 ml (14 fl oz) tinned coconut cream

350 g (12 oz) frozen peeled and deveined raw prawns (shrimp)

1¼ cups (100 g) baby spinach leaves

juice of 1 lime

1 handful coriander (cilantro) leaves, finely chopped

SERVES 2–4

I try to have a packet of prawns stashed in the freezer at all times. Whenever the fridge is looking bare, I remember them and suddenly all sorts of dinner options are back on the table, including this delicious curry. Full of creamy, coconutty southern Indian flavours and whipped together on one oven tray, it's perfect midweek fare.

I'm very happy for you to throw the prawns into the curry while still frozen, saving yourself the time and hassle of defrosting (or defrost them using the tips below). Just be sure to use deveined raw prawns, with or without the tail intact.

Preheat the oven to 180°C (350°F).

Combine the tomatoes, capsicum, onion, ginger, spices, curry leaves, salt and oil in a roasting tin and mix thoroughly to coat everything evenly. Roast for 15–20 minutes, checking after 15 minutes, giving everything a good stir and adding a splash of water if it looks like it's drying out and starting to char.

Remove the tin from the oven and press down on the cherry tomatoes with the back of a wooden spoon to squash them and spread their juices over the other ingredients. Add the coconut cream, prawns and spinach, and give everything a good stir, then return to the oven for a further 8–10 minutes, or until the prawns are pink and just cooked through. Remove from the oven.

Squeeze over the lime juice, scatter over the coriander and season to taste with salt. Perfect served with rice or flatbreads.

1. To defrost prawns quickly, place them in a large colander under cold running water for a few minutes, moving them around as you go so they defrost evenly. Do not use warm water, which will defrost the prawns unevenly and can even start cooking them on the outside.

2. I love to use fresh curry leaves, as I have a monster tree in the garden and I'm always looking for ways to use them, but they're not essential. If you can't get hold of them easily or dried are the only option available, then just leave them out.

Okay, this recipe is BULLSHIT easy. – Yumi

Gyoza Goals

SERVES 2

Gyoza used to be such a going-out treat, but there are now multiple options in the freezer section of the supermarket for cooking at home. Something that can feed your family that's easy and tasty and can live in your freezer? That's a win as far as I'm concerned. The thing is, they're actually a little bit tricky to get right, and they need to be cooked from frozen, meaning you can sometimes burn the outside while the inside remains stone-cold. To get the most out of your store-bought gyoza, here's what to do.

Steaming method
This is the most reliable way to cook gyoza.

Set a steamer over a saucepan half full of boiling water over medium heat. If it's a metal steamer, grease it with the grapeseed oil or spray it lightly with cooking oil spray. Place the gyoza in the steamer, cover with the lid, and cook for the time recommended in the packet directions.

Frying pan method
This can be the trickiest way to cook gyoza but will give the most satisfying results. As you are cooking from frozen, if you fry too hot, the outside will burn while the inside will still be frozen. Aim for a medium–low heat and be patient. Preheat the pan, add the oil, and spread the gyoza out so they have a little space. Put the lid on the frying pan, as it will stop spatters and create a steamy environment, allowing the gyoza to cook all over.

For best results, aim only to fry the flattest side. Once it has reached a nice golden-brown colour, add about 3 teaspoons water to the pan, shut the lid quickly, and allow the steam to cook the other parts of the gyoza.

Frying pan method with lattice
Mix the lattice ingredients together in a small jug.

Fry seven gyoza in 2 tablespoons of oil, arranging them on their flat sides so that they will fit perfectly onto a specific serving plate. When the dumplings develop an appealing golden burnish on their flat side (as in the frying pan method), pour the lattice ingredients all around the gyoza, but not over them. Wait 5–6 minutes, or until the lattice has cooked and turned golden and crispy. It takes longer than you might think.

Put your chosen serving plate face down on the dumplings then flip the whole lot over onto the plate, and serve.

Dipping sauce
To make the dipping sauce, combine all the ingredients in a small bowl and whisk with a fork.

14 frozen gyoza
(about 360 g/12¾ oz)

2–3 tablespoons grapeseed oil,
or cooking oil spray

DIPPING SAUCE

2 tablespoons soy sauce

2 tablespoons rice wine vinegar
or Chinkiang vinegar

½ teaspoon sesame oil

chopped red chilli, to taste,
or 1 teaspoon sambal oelek
(optional)

LATTICE (FOR 7 GYOZA)

4 teaspoons plain (all-purpose) flour

¼ cup (50 ml) water

pinch of salt

The lattice is so worth the effort. Do it! — SIMON

1 Rice flour works really well here, but it doesn't colour, and it forms a crunchier but less detailed lattice.

2 If you want more than seven gyoza in your lattice, you can definitely add more, but don't let it get crowded past, say, twelve. If working in batches, it's okay to scale up the lattice ingredients, but be sure to stir the mixture well before pouring because the flour will settle to the bottom of the mixture.

Simon's Fish Finger Sandwich

SERVES 2

10 fish fingers

4 slices wholemeal or white bread

4–6 little gem lettuce leaves, washed

8 cherry tomatoes, cut into quarters

Quick-pickled Red Onions (page 214; optional)

tomato ketchup, to serve (optional)

CHEAT'S TARTARE

8–10 cornichons or 3–4 gherkins (pickles), finely chopped

½ cup (130 g) Greek-style yoghurt

juice of ½ lemon

salt and pepper

No, fish don't *actually* have fingers but yes, dinner can be a sandwich and yes, said digits can be delicious. The cheat's tartare is one of my yoghurty sauces that can be made in seconds and delivers so much bright flavour and creaminess to the party that I actually much prefer it to the mayonnaise equivalent. Serve with a mountain of buttered boiled (frozen) peas and a few golden oven chips for the full experience.

Preheat the oven to 220°C (425°F).

Arrange the fish fingers on a baking tray in a single even layer, allowing plenty of space between them. Whack in the oven and cook for 15–20 minutes, turning carefully at the halfway stage, until the fingers are beautifully burnished and bronzed.

Meanwhile, prepare the rest. For the cheat's tartare, combine the cornichons or gherkins with the yoghurt and lemon juice and mix thoroughly. Season with a little salt (no need for a lot here as the pickles are salty) and a good grind of pepper, then taste and adjust the seasoning as needed, adding a squeeze more lemon juice if you like things a little brighter/sharper.

Lightly toast the bread until ever so slightly coloured but still retaining a little softness. (You're looking to avoid the rigidity of full-on toasted toast.) Slather each slice with a generous layer of the tartare sauce.

Remove the fish fingers from the oven and arrange them in neat vertical lines on two of the toast slices. Top with the lettuce leaves, cherry tomatoes and quick-pickled red onion, if using, then cover with the remaining toast. Cut in half with a sharp knife, then transfer to plates and serve with the excess tartare sauce and ketchup, if you like, for dipping the edges of the sandwich into as you go.

One time Simon and I had a 'work' meeting at a cafe and there was a fish finger sandwich on the menu and he told me not to order it 'cos their version was crap. Lol. — Yumi

1. Trust me, not much can make this sandwich better. Fancy sourdough bread? Nope. Home-crumbed fish goujons? Definitely not. It's a dish that embraces its humble ingredients. Go with it.

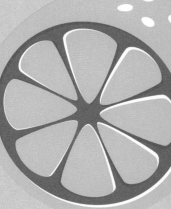

174

Berries with Hot White Chocolate Sauce

SERVES 4–6

2 cups (250 g) small frozen mixed berries (e.g. blueberries, raspberries, redcurrants)

150 g (5½ oz) good-quality white chocolate, roughly chopped

150 ml (5 fl oz) thick (double) cream

2 teaspoons vanilla extract

When you need dessert in seconds but it still has to be impressive and utterly delicious, it's impossible to go past this. I can't take any credit for this recipe, which was a mainstay on British chef Mark Hix's London restaurant menus in the early noughties – and which had apparently been given to him by a customer who had it in Scandinavia and was raving about it – but I can tell you that you will find no better use for that bag of frozen berries you have lurking in your freezer. Icy-cold fruit and molten, creamy chocolate sauce? It's criminally simple and as good as it gets.

Five minutes before serving, divide the berries among serving plates or ramekins and leave at room temperature to lose a little of their chill.

Put the chocolate, cream and vanilla in a bowl and place over a saucepan of lightly simmering water, ensuring the bowl doesn't touch the water. Whisk together until the chocolate has melted.

Pour the hot chocolate sauce over the berries (you can do this either in the kitchen or theatrically at the table from a serving jug) and serve immediately.

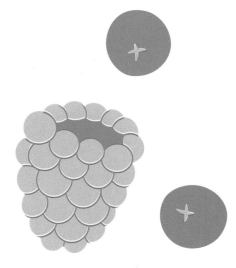

1 You can use pretty much any berries you like here, as long as they are small. A pack of mixed frozen berries works well, but be sure to fish the strawberries out, as they turn mushy when they come into contact with the hot chocolate sauce.

L–R: Instant Banana Ice Cream (page 178), Berries with Hot White Chocolate Sauce, Magical Milo Ice Cream (page 179).

Instant Banana Ice Cream

4–6 ripe bananas

1 tablespoon honey

½ teaspoon ground cardamom or ground cinnamon

2–3 speculoos or speculaas biscuits

SERVES 4–6

This is barely a recipe at all, but the end result is so very good – and it's such a ridiculously brilliant way to get through those overripe bananas we all have lurking in the fruit bowl from time to time – that I had to include it.

I've included instructions for prepping and freezing the bananas as you go here, but I actually do that bit whenever I have bananas on the turn. Then it's just a matter of whipping the bag out of the freezer and using them straight away. This can be as simple as just bananas, but I do like to sneak in the additional flavourings to make it just that little bit more amazing. (Pictured on page 177.)

Peel the bananas, cut them in 5–7.5 cm (2–3 inch) chunks and place them in a freezer bag in the freezer for at least 6 hours.

Pop the frozen banana in a high-speed blender or food processor, add the other ingredients and blend until smooth. Serve immediately, or freeze in an airtight container for at least 2 hours then thaw for 2 minutes. Scoop and serve.

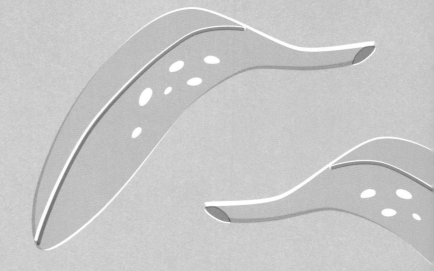

1   If you like your ice cream with more of a soft-serve consistency, add a few tablespoons of milk (or coconut milk) to the blender before whizzing. A handful of raw cashews makes a lovely addition.

2   If you want to take this in a slightly different direction, try replacing the biscuits and spices with ¼ cup (30 g) chocolate chips, 2 tablespoons crunchy peanut butter and ½ teaspoon vanilla extract.

Magical Milo Ice Cream

MAKES ABOUT 500 G (1 LB 2 OZ)

Home-made ice cream is a tricky thing. First you have to make egg-based custard on the stove, with lots of stirring and gentle cooking, then there's a whole lot more fiddling and fussing as it freezes – pulling it out regularly and beating to prevent ice crystals forming so you get a nice smooth texture (unless you've dropped a shedload of cash on a fancy-pants ice-cream machine, that is).

This recipe has none of that – just 5 minutes prep, shove it in the freezer and forget about it. Thanks to the sweetened condensed milk, those pesky ice crystals don't form, leaving you with a super-delicious sweet frozen treat without any of the usual faff. It's very rich, so best enjoyed in small doses, but the malty Milo flavour is a real crowd-pleaser. (Pictured on page 177.)

Pour the condensed milk and cream into a large mixing bowl, add the Milo and whisk together until the mixture forms 'loose peaks' – i.e. it holds its shape for a little while after whisking. (The best way to test it is to lift your whisk and let a little of the mixture drip back into the bowl; if it piles up on top and stays there for a second or two before being swallowed back up, you're good to go.)

Pour into an airtight container and freeze for 8 hours.

When ready to serve, scoop the ice cream into small bowls. Serve straight up or with mango or berries to cut through the rich sweetness and a topping of Maltesers or pretzels for texture.

200 g (7 oz) sweetened condensed milk

300 ml (10½ fl oz) thick (double) cream

¼ cup (30 g) Milo (or other chocolate malted drink powder, such as Horlicks or Ovaltine)

TO SERVE (OPTIONAL)

mango or berries

Maltesers or pretzel bites

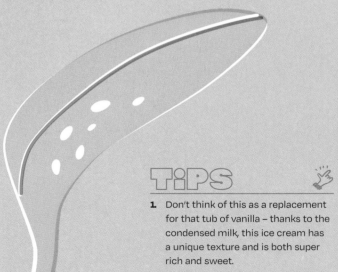

TiPS

1. Don't think of this as a replacement for that tub of vanilla – thanks to the condensed milk, this ice cream has a unique texture and is both super rich and sweet.

2. For a lemony twist, try replacing the Milo with a sharp lemon curd. Serve with summer berries and crushed meringue.

DON'T

THE SWEE

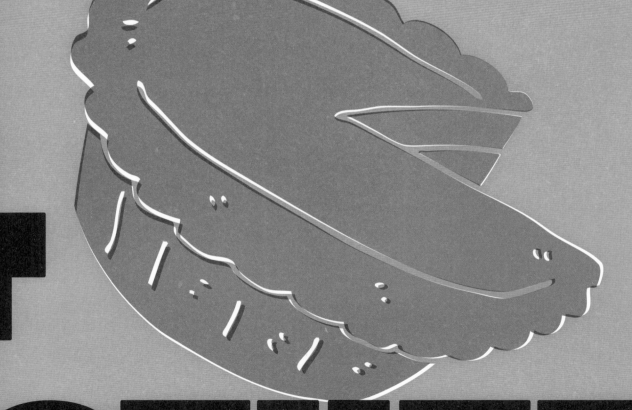

Killer Spiced Fruit Crumble

6 cardamom pods

800 g (1 lb 12 oz) ripe stonefruit, such as peaches, nectarines or plums, halved and stones removed

50 g (1¾ oz) soft brown sugar

finely grated zest of 1 orange

1 teaspoon ground cinnamon

1 teaspoon plain (all-purpose) flour

whipped cream, to serve

CRUMBLE TOPPING

100 g (3½ oz) crisp amaretti biscuits

150 g (5½ oz) plain (all-purpose) flour

80 g (2¾ oz) caster (superfine) sugar

80 g (2¾ oz) light muscovado sugar

¼ cup (25 g) rolled oats

150 g (5½ oz) butter, melted

Who doesn't love a crumble? Well, my kids for a start, but that's not a problem ... all the more for me.

A few things tip this over from an ordinary crumble into slightly special territory. First there are the spices for the stone fruit. You could just use ground cinnamon, but if you give a few cardamom pods a bash, you'll have something far more exciting. The same with the amaretti biscuits in the crumble (we're after the crispy, crunchy ones, not the soft ones): while the crumble would still be lovely without them, they certainly make things more interesting. And if the kids aren't going to eat it anyway, then why not?

Preheat the oven to 200°C (400°F).

Using the end of a rolling pin, bash the cardamom pods to split them open and remove the seeds. Place the seeds in a pestle and mortar and grind to a rough powder.

Place the fruit in a 20 x 30 cm (8 x 12 inch) baking dish and add the sugar, orange zest, cinnamon, cardamom powder and flour, then toss everything together to combine.

Roast in the oven for 20 minutes, or until the fruit has softened.

Meanwhile, make the crumble topping. Put the amaretti biscuits in a snaplock bag and bash with the rolling pin until finely crushed (or pulse them briefly in a food processor), then tip into a medium bowl and stir in the flour, sugars and rolled oats. Add the butter and combine with the dry ingredients to form a crumble.

Scatter the crumble topping over the roasted fruit and pop back in the oven for 20–25 minutes, or until golden and bubbling. Serve warm with whipped cream.

1. If you're used to making crumble, you'll see that there's no rubbing cold cubed butter into the dry ingredients here – instead we're just stirring everything together. While this might horrify purists, it still gives a great result but with minimum fuss.

Baked Custard

720 ml (24 fl oz) milk

1 pandan leaf (optional)

1 teaspoon vanilla essence

6 eggs

140 g (5 oz) caster (superfine) sugar

freshly grated nutmeg, to taste, and/
or 2 tablespoons cinnamon sugar

As a kid, I ordered a custard tart from the tuckshop every day, then spooned the custard out of the pastry, relishing the nutmeggy goodness and the soothing, puddingy texture, but not really liking the pastry shell which had that soulless industrial-baking vibe and left me feeling regretful if I ate it. Ever since, I've longed for a simple custard that didn't require stirring, didn't call for egg yolks only (because what would I do with the whites?), wasn't too stodgy and, most of all, didn't require a pastry that usually involved the most work for the poorest return. This is the recipe I've been waiting for my whole life!

I'd love to take credit for it, but Cornersmith's cookbook *The Food Saver's A-Z* includes this wonderful recipe, which apparently came from Tasmanian farmer/chef Matthew Evans. Naturally, I have made some customisations.

Preheat the oven to 150°C (300°F), get the kettle on the boil and check that you have a baking dish that will fit inside a high-sided roasting tray.

Pour the milk into a medium saucepan. If using the pandan leaf, tie it in a knot and crush it a little, then add to the pan with the vanilla. Bring to a gentle simmer over medium–low heat, then remove from the heat.

Using an electric mixer, whisk the eggs with the sugar at low speed until just combined. Pluck the pandan leaf out of the milk and discard, then with the mixer running, slowly pour the milk into the egg mixture. Mix until the sugar has dissolved.

Tip the whole lot through a strainer directly into the baking dish, then top with freshly grated nutmeg and/or cinnamon sugar. (I like to really carpet the top with sugary cinnamon, but perhaps showing restraint here could be classy ... how would I know?)

Carefully place the baking dish in the roasting tin, then carefully pour a kettle full of boiling water into the roasting tin, so that the baking dish is sitting in a bath of hot water. Bake for 30–40 minutes, until softly set. Serve hot – delicious. Serve cold – delicious.

TIPS

1. I use lactose-free milk for this, which makes the whole thing less taxing on my digestion.

2. You can buy cinnamon sugar already made up but it's cheaper to make it yourself just by blending 1:1 cinnamon and caster sugar.

3. Experiment with flavours. The dish will not gravely suffer for not having pandan leaf so don't worry if you can't get any. You might want to try saffron or cardamom, or a handful of sultanas cooked with the milk.

Apple Pie with Cheddar

SERVES 4–6

You may not have heard of this combination before, but it's a thing and that thing is superb. In fact, apple pie and cheese have a long history – in the north of England a slice of pie is often served with a wedge of sharp, tangy Wensleydale, while in parts of the States (particularly the Midwest) a pie is just not complete unless it's crowned with a slice of radiant, Trumpian orange dairy. The combination makes sense, of course – just think of that slice of apple on a cheese board or ploughman's.

Preheat the oven to 220°C (425°F). Grease a 23 cm (9 inch) pie tin with oil.

Peel and core the apples and cut into 5 mm (¼ inch) slices.

Mix the sugar, flour, nutmeg, cinnamon and salt together in a large bowl. Add the apples and stir to coat.

Lay a puff pastry sheet on the benchtop, scatter half the grated cheddar over, then fold in half. On a lightly floured surface, roll out to 5 mm (¼ inch) thick with a rolling pin. Repeat with the remaining puff pastry sheet and cheese. Use one sheet of the pastry to line the prepared pie tin, trimming away the excess.

Spoon the apple mixture into the lined pie tin and dot with the butter. Cover with the remaining puff pastry sheet, trimming away the excess and pinching the edges of the two sheets together to seal. Cut slits in the top (to allow the steam to escape and prevent the pastry going soggy). Brush the pastry lightly with beaten egg.

Bake for 40–50 minutes until the pastry is golden and the juices are bubbling through the slits. Remove from the oven and leave to cool slightly before serving with custard or vanilla ice cream.

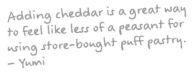

Adding cheddar is a great way to feel like less of a peasant for using store-bought puff pastry.
— Yumi

vegetable oil or cooking oil spray, for greasing

8 cooking apples (such as granny smith or bramley)

⅔ cup (150 g) caster (superfine) sugar

¼ cup (35 g) self-raising flour

½ teaspoon ground nutmeg

½ teaspoon ground cinnamon

pinch of salt

2 sheets frozen puff pastry

2 cups (200 g) grated mature cheddar cheese

2 tablespoons butter, diced

1 egg, beaten

custard or vanilla ice cream, to serve

TIPS

1 If you really want to ramp up the umami, you can use parmesan cheese instead of cheddar.

2 If the pie seems to be browning too quickly, cover the outer 5 cm (2 inches) with a strip of foil.

Banoffee Pie, Two Ways

SERVES 6

¼ cup (40 g) pepitas (pumpkin seeds), toasted

cooking oil spray, for greasing

⅓ cup (60 g) soft pitted dates, halved

75 g (2¾ oz) butter

250 g (9 oz) choc ripple biscuits or other chocolate-flavoured (not choc-coated) biscuits

600 ml (21 fl oz) thick (double) cream

1 tablespoon honey or caster (superfine) sugar

dulce de leche (page 211)

6 ripe but firm bananas

dark chocolate, to garnish

Banoffee pie celebrates the humble banana and adds two wonderful and simple ingredients: freshly whipped cream, and dulce de leche. This is super easy to throw together, particularly if you've been clever and already have several cans of dulce de leche on standby.

My darling friend Carla has shown up and been there for every major life event of mine for more than 20 years. She has taught me how to be a good friend through years of patient, loving, continuous demonstration. While she shows her love by showing up, I show mine by feeding people. On one of Carla's birthdays I made this for her, knowing that banana desserts and honey desserts are two of her favourite things in the world.

Preheat the oven to 150°C (300°F).

(If you haven't already toasted the pepitas for 7–10 minutes, you can do that now.)

Lightly grease a 24 cm (9½ inch) round shallow pie tin with cooking oil spray.

Put the dates and butter together in a small ceramic dish and put it in the microwave for 40–50 seconds to melt the butter. (This will also soften the dates, but be careful not to burn them by boiling the butter.)

Empty the biscuits into a food processor. Whiz to crumbs, then with the motor still running, add the pepitas and pour in the date butter mixture, whizzing until everything is well mixed to fine wet crumbs.

Tip the whole lot into the pie tin and shape into a crust with clean hands, pressing the mixture up the sides and flattening and compressing it on the base with your hands or a jar. Cover the crust with baking paper, top the paper with baking beads, uncooked rice or dried beans and blind bake for 10 minutes.

Remove from the oven, take away the baking beads and baking paper and allow the crust to cool. This is now most of the work done. (This crust can also be used for cheesecake – it's very good.)

Using an electric mixer with the whisk attachment, beat the cream together with the honey to soft peaks.

Spread the bottom and sides of the pie crust with a whole tin of dulce de leche. Top with the whipped cream. Slice the banana and decorate the pie with masses of it. Garnish with a fine grating of dark chocolate. Serve within the day.

Deconstructed Banoffee Pie

dulce de leche (page 211)

shop-bought flat ice-cream wafers

freshly whipped cream

ripe but firm bananas

good-quality dark chocolate

For me, the problem with making banoffee pie is that the crust is the least interesting part, but requires the most work. Deconstructing it gives you all the best parts with none of the boring bits.

Spread dulce de leche on each wafer. Top with a 1.5 cm (⅝ inch) layer of whipped cream. Press in slices of banana. (I love lots of banana, but it tends to fall off and make a mess – which is part of the fun.) Grate dark chocolate over and serve immediately.

Fully Loaded Banana Bread

1 teaspoon bicarbonate of soda
(baking soda)

1 cup (260 g) Greek-style yoghurt

100 g (3½ oz) butter, melted

1 cup (220 g) caster (superfine) sugar

2 eggs

1⅔ cups (250 g) plain
(all-purpose) flour

1 teaspoon baking powder

1 teaspoon ground cinnamon

400 g (14 oz) mashed ripe banana
(from 4–5 bananas)

TOPPING (OPTIONAL)

¼ cup (45 g) lightly packed
brown sugar

⅓ cup (35 g) flaked almonds

With three small people in the house, we're pretty used to having the ground constantly shifting under our feet. Favourite foods chop and change in the blink of an eye (seriously, sometimes over the course of one meal) and keeping up as we try to go about the daily routine of making sure everyone is still alive and nourished can be something of a struggle. Thankfully, some things stay the same – we always have a ton of bananas in the house and some will *always* go brown. When enough of them do, we turn to this banana bread. The fact that it always goes down well is a miracle.

Preheat the oven to 180°C (350°F). Grease and line a 900 g (2 lb) loaf tin with baking paper.

For the topping (if making), mix the brown sugar and almonds in a small bowl. Set aside.

In a large bowl, mix together the bicarbonate of soda and yoghurt, then leave to sit for 5 minutes for the soda to work its magic.

Stir the melted butter, sugar and eggs into the yoghurt mixture, then add the flour, baking powder and cinnamon and fold in gently to form a batter. Tip in the mashed banana and mix together gently to combine, then spoon the batter into the prepared tin.

Sprinkle the sugar and almond topping over the top, transfer to the oven and bake for 1½ hours, or until a skewer inserted into the middle of the loaf comes out clean. Cool in the tin for 5 minutes, then transfer to a wire rack and leave to cool completely.

TIPS

1. The topping is really delicious and gives the banana bread a lovely crackly crumb, but it's also entirely optional – the loaf is perfectly tasty without it.

2. Don't throw away the banana skins – instead, pop them in a large jar or container, cover with water and leave for 2–3 days before tipping the water over your favourite plants and putting the drained skins in the compost. You get to feel smug that you've used the whole banana and your plant gets a boost from all that potassium and other nutrients in the banana 'tea'. Win-win.

IO TIPS
FOR COOKING FOR A SPECIAL OCCASION

Cooking for a birthday or Christmas, or just having friends over, is one of the joys of adulthood. It's celebrating the loved ones in your life in your own space, where you get to do things at your own pace, unbothered by restaurant closing times, weather or the need to wear underpants.
To ensure success:

I.

Put all dishes away and clean the kitchen so you have a blank canvas before people arrive. Yes, mess will be made, so start off tidy.

2.

Write a list of what you need, the menu you're serving and any other key tasks for the day so that you're not constantly going over everything in your head.

3.

Set yourself up to succeed. Don't make any food that requires precision or constant attention. Serve dishes you've successfully made before.

4.

Before the day, check in with your friends and ask them, 'What time do you like to eat?' I'll never forget being at a friend's house for dinner and an hour after I arrived she put a meal in the oven that was going to take three hours to cook. I was so hungry and so dismayed.

5.

Sometimes in life throwing money at a problem works. It's okay to buy great bread, fancy ice cream, a gorgeous cake, smoked salmon, oysters and cheese.

6.

Delegate drinks to someone who's keen. That doesn't have to be your job.

7.

In the week leading up to the party, I like to run down supplies of other stuff so there's room in the fridge for the stars of the show.

8.

Simon insists on putting a drink and a snack in the hands of his guests within a minute or two of their arrival. It sets them at ease and makes for a great experience (and makes you a great host).

9.

Take it easy. No one wants to see you frazzled and shitty. They're there to enjoy you (and, you know, Christmas or whatever), not be wowed by some haute cuisine nonsense. Be radiant. Serve slops.

IO.

In the interests of saving the planet and reducing food waste, it's perfectly okay to encourage your friends to bring their own containers so they can take leftovers home.

Freeform Fig Tart

SERVES 6

Nothing puts a full stop on a fantastic meal quite like a bejewelled, glistening, fruit-laden tart. I love the rustic nature of tarts like this – there's magic in the uneven folds, and to my mind, they look better than their rigid, casebound cousins.

The idea of making your own pastry may be enough to send you running for the hills, but this one isn't hard. Based on a sour cream pastry recipe by Maggie Beer, it's foolproof, comes together in the food processor in under a minute, is incredibly crumbly and delicious, and is also extremely versatile, working well in both sweet and savoury dishes.

To make the pastry, dice the butter, then pulse with the flour in a food processor until the mixture resembles fine breadcrumbs. Add the sour cream and continue to pulse until the dough starts to form a ball. Wrap the dough in plastic wrap and refrigerate for at least 20 minutes.

While the pastry is chilling, cut the tips off the figs and discard, then cut the figs into quarters.

When you are ready to make the tart, preheat the oven to 190°C (375°F). Line a large baking tray with baking paper.

Roll out the chilled pastry into a rough circle about 35 cm (14 inches) in diameter and 3 mm (⅛ inch) thick. Transfer the dough to the prepared baking tray and spread the marmalade over the surface, leaving a 5 cm (2 inch) border.

Arrange the fig quarters in the centre of the pastry in a circular pattern, again leaving a 5 cm (2 inch) border. Sprinkle the sugar over the figs, then fold the edge of the pastry towards the centre so that it sits up and over the edges of the filling, tucking everything in nicely. Roughly pleat the crust edges, brush the pastry with beaten egg, then bake for 45–50 minutes, until the crust is lightly browned and the fruit is bubbling.

Remove from the oven and leave to cool for 30 minutes before serving.

500 g (1 lb 2 oz) figs
¼ cup (85 g) orange marmalade
1 tablespoon caster (superfine) sugar

SOUR CREAM PASTRY
200 g (7 oz) cold butter
250 g (7 oz) plain (all-purpose) flour
½ cup (125 g) sour cream
1 egg, beaten

This is genuinely amazing. Don't serve it to anyone you hate. — Yumi

1. You might be tempted to load up the tart with extra figs, but trust me, just like when you're filling a burrito, less is more. The figs release quite a bit of juice, which can leak and make a mess of the crust and your oven if you go OTT.

2. Pears, plums and apricots will all give delicious results. Just be sure to use ripe fruit and cut them into pieces roughly the same size as a quartered fig. The marmalade can be replaced with any jam you have to hand.

3. This tart is best served warm but is also great at room temperature. It will keep covered in the fridge for up to 2 days – leave to stand at room temperature for about 30 minutes before serving.

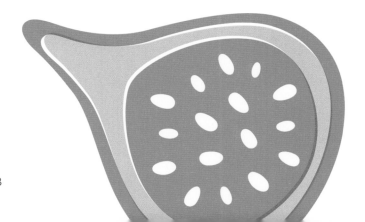

1¼ cups (310 fl oz) milk

½ cup (110 g) sugar

1 teaspoon vanilla essence

⅓ cup (60 g) sultanas

½ cup (95 g) semolina

1½ teaspoons ground cardamom

3 tablespoons ghee

1 handful slivered almonds, toasted (optional)

Seriously moreish. I could eat this for breakfast (and have). — Simon

Sooji Halwa: Sweet Semolina

SERVES 4

This recipe should be taught in Pleasure School. When I found it in a cookbook called *Pass it On*, by New Zealanders Shobha and Keryn Kalyan, I was deeply delighted (I'd eaten it many times but never knew how to make it). The authors are a mother-daughter duo who are 4th generation Kiwis and use traditional Indian recipes just the way their older generations used to. Here, your semolina will be soft, puddingy and porridgey, with intriguing textural complexity. Kids like it too, and it can be eaten hot or cold. There's nothing tricky in the cooking method and the results are so yummy that this is one recipe I beg you to try. Gently dry-frying the semolina before adding the liquid unleashes a toasty, nutty aroma and the cardamom is delightful.

Heat the milk, sugar, vanilla and sultanas in a small saucepan over medium heat until starting to foam. Remove from the heat.

Heat a skillet or frying pan over medium heat and add the semolina and cardamom. Cook for 3 minutes, stirring to make sure the semolina burnishes evenly; it should change colour and release a delightful aroma.

Add the ghee, which should froth and bubble, and fry the semolina until golden brown all through. Gradually add the milk, stirring to incorporate it until absorbed. The mixture should be porridge-like, so if it cooks too fast and starts to look crumbly and dry, add more milk, ¼ cup (60 ml) at a time.

To serve, spoon into bowls and top with the almonds.

Weekly Cupcakes

MAKES 12

I make these once a week to keep up a constant supply. The fussy kid loves them. The garbage-guts kid loves them. Adults love them. I don't ice them 'cos they don't need it, and I keep extras in the freezer so I always have some to pop into lunchboxes or – get this – the microwave, where they turn puddingy and molten and squishy and go perfectly with vanilla ice cream and fresh cream. It's an excellent short-notice dessert.

This recipe also appeared in my last book, and in honour of its publication here I've given the option of making it as one big cake.

Preheat the oven to 175°C (350°F). Line a 12-hole cupcake tin with paper cases.

Put the butter in a large bowl and break the chocolate into the same bowl. Set aside.

In a small saucepan, combine the cornflour, cocoa powder, brown sugar and water. Whisk well then place over medium heat, whisking constantly until the mixture turns thick and glossy. Still whisking, remove from the heat, then pour into the bowl with the butter and chocolate and stir until both melt into the mixture.

Tip the whole lot into the bowl of an electric mixer with the whisk attachment. Give it a couple of minutes to cool, then add the oil, vanilla, baking powder and caster sugar and mix well. Add the eggs one at a time, mixing well after each addition to incorporate completely. Sift in the flour and fold in using a large metal spoon until just combined.

Scoop the batter into the prepared paper cases. Bake for 15 minutes. When the cupcakes are set on top (no wobble, no sink), remove from the oven and cool completely on a wire rack.

Eat immediately, no icing necessary.

One big cake?
Use two 20 cm (4 inch) springform cake tins lined with baking paper and divide the batter between them. Cook for 15 minutes, being careful to check they're cooking evenly. (I've had failures where the one on the lower shelf didn't cook in the middle but I only checked the one on the higher shelf.) Allow the cakes to cool before sandwiching them together with 300 ml (10½ fl oz) thick (double) cream whipped with 2 teaspoons caster (superfine) sugar.

75 g (2¾ oz) butter

125 g (4½ oz) good-quality 75% cocoa dark chocolate

50 g (1¾ oz) cornflour (cornstarch)

¼ cup (30 g) unsweetened cocoa powder

½ cup (100 g) soft brown sugar

225 ml (7½ fl oz) cold water

75 ml (2½ fl oz) grapeseed oil

2 teaspoons vanilla essence

2 teaspoons baking powder

125 g (4½ oz) caster (superfine) sugar

2 eggs

½ cup (125 g) plain (all-purpose) flour

My kids love these too. And so do I! – SIMON

TiPS

1. I always use a double layer of paper cases because the one nearest the cake tends to get oily.

2. I tried to care about icing but they don't need it.

Carrot Cake with Olive Oil Icing

SERVES 5–6

1 large egg, at room temperature

⅔ cup (150 g) caster (superfine) sugar

1½ tablespoons non-fat buttermilk, at room temperature

150 g (5½ oz) carrots, finely grated

½ cup (125 ml) extra virgin olive oil, plus extra for drizzling

1 cup (150 g) plain (all-purpose) flour, plus extra for dusting

¾ teaspoon baking powder

⅓ teaspoon bicarbonate of soda (baking soda)

¼ teaspoon salt

carrot ribbons or carrot tops, to serve (optional)

OLIVE OIL ICING

1 cup (125 g) icing (confectioners') sugar

⅓ cup (80 ml) extra virgin olive oil

One of the incredible chefs I've worked with in my day job is the amazing California-based Kevin O'Connor. His cooking has a nomadic spirit and a love for seasonal produce, cooked simply and without fuss but with a whole lot of heart and with a deep understanding of ingredients and flavour. His recipe for carrot cake with olive oil icing blew me away. It's a great example of how a genius chef can look at a classic in a new light and create something exceptionally delicious. And – in this case – it's incredibly easy to make at home, too.

Preheat the oven to 160°C (315°F).

Grease an 18 cm (7 inch) round cake tin with a drizzle of olive oil. Dust with flour and tap out any excess. Set aside.

Whisk the egg and sugar together in a large bowl until pale and creamy. Whisk in the buttermilk, carrots and olive oil.

In a separate medium bowl, whisk together the flour, baking powder, bicarbonate of soda and salt.

Stir the flour mixture into the carrot mixture until completely combined, then transfer the batter to the prepared tin and bake for 45–50 minutes, or until a skewer inserted in the centre comes out clean.

Meanwhile, make the icing by vigorously whisking the icing sugar and olive oil together until thoroughly combined.

Remove the cake from the oven and turn out onto a wire rack to cool completely, then spread the icing over the top. Decorate with carrot ribbons or carrot tops, if you like.

1. It's really, really important you use extra virgin olive oil here and not the mild, regular stuff. That's because all the lovely punchy, peppery flavours that the oil lends to the buttercream dressing and the cake are taking the place of the usual spices in a carrot cake. Without a tasty oil, this isn't going to taste half as great as it should.

Adzuki Beans with Mochi

I've had a blast teaching this recipe to a friend's teenage son. Like a lot of Aussie kids, he loves Asian sweets, and while this one seems exotic, it's easy. *Easy.* My hope is when I'm long gone he'll still be making this and one day teaching it to his teenage grandkids.

Ridiculously enjoyable to both eat and create are the little white dumplings to go in the beans. These mochi are almost completely flavourless, but are all about texture. They're also shockingly easy to make with glutinous rice flour, which is widely available. Eating the dumplings is a lip-smacking sensory experience designed for nothing but mouthfeel and yums.

To remove the bitter protective chemical in the adzuki bean skin, put the beans in a saucepan, cover generously with water, and bring to the boil over medium heat. As soon as it boils, drain the beans in a sieve and rinse under cold water, before returning them to the empty pot. Cover well with more water, then bring to the boil over medium heat. Reduce the heat to low and simmer for 40 minutes. (The exact cooking time will depend on the bean but I find Australian-grown adzuki beans don't need much longer than that. If you can easily crush a bean between your forefinger and thumb, they're ready.)

Add the sugar and a pinch of salt to the beans. Top up with more water if it looks like it's drying out – the texture should be somewhere between porridge and pumpkin soup – and cook for 10 more minutes. (You could strain the finished sweetened beans to get rid of the skins and smooth out the texture but the fibre is good for you, the texture is interesting and life is short, so we're not doing that.)

To make the mochi balls, bring a small saucepan of water to the boil, and prepare an ice bath (a bowl of cold water with a cup of ice cubes in it). In a small bowl, mix the water into the glutinous rice flour until it forms a stiff dough with no floury lumps. This only takes a second, and the dough should be easy to handle. Roll into 10 g (¼ oz) balls (slightly bigger than a Malteser but smaller than a Lindt ball). Drop them into the boiling water. Once they float, give them another 30 seconds then scoop them straight out and into the ice bath. Leave to cool for a minute and then remove. This recipe should make 20–24 balls.

To serve, portion out about ½ cup cooked adzuki beans per person then top with 5–6 mochi balls. The left-over adzuki beans will last in an airtight container in the fridge for more than 1 week and in the freezer for 3 months.

250 g (9 oz) dried adzuki beans
160 g (5¾ oz) brown sugar
pinch of salt

MOCHI BALLS
100 ml (3½ fl oz) water
120 g (4¼ oz) glutinous rice flour

FOOD G
&
ESSE

PiCKLES

FTS
ANTRY
NTiALS

Wedding-guest Croutons

MAKES 3 LARGE SERVES

400 g (14 oz) sourdough bread (stale leftovers if possible)

⅓ cup (80 ml) olive oil

1 teaspoon finely grated or chopped garlic

2 tablespoons dried herbs (e.g. parsley, oregano, mint)

1 teaspoon salt

Should be called crack croutons. Put on everything. — SIMON

One day a co-worker started snacking on the croutons another co-worker had brought from home. 'They're just so good!' she said. Turns out it was my recipe. I had no recollection of sharing the recipe or even *having* a recipe for croutons, but of course I loved them sick and was happy to bask in the reflected glory. The thing I do recall is deep contemplation of the crouton. It must be like the perfect wedding guest. In other words, it's not the bride in any salad or soup scenario. No one wants the best man to be more charismatic than the groom, or the mother of the bride to be sexier than the bride. A crouton needs to know its place, but also how to party – and these are lit. They'll improve any salad or soup. Or try them on Simon's Pan Con Tomate (page 69).

Preheat the oven to 180°C (350°F) and have a couple of baking trays at the ready.

Cut the bread into 1.5 cm (⅝ inch) cubes. Don't overthink it. They don't need to match or look neat, uniform or in any way perfect. Just cut 'em up and chuck 'em in a large bowl like you're time-poor. The croutons will be fine.

In a small bowl, mix the oil, garlic, dried herbs and salt. Give them a good stir then pour the mixture over the bread. Mix everything with your hands, squeezing the oil into the bread and crushing the drier cubes of bread into the oily ones.

Tumble the bread out onto the oven trays and spread them into an uncrowded single layer. Bake for 10 minutes, stir, then bake again. Keep an eye on them. They're ready when they're golden brown, crunchy and smelling amazing. Once completely cooled, store in an airtight jar or container in the pantry for up to 2 weeks.

TIPS

1. The better the bread, the better the crouton.

2. These are meant to be moreish. If not, you might have done something wrong.

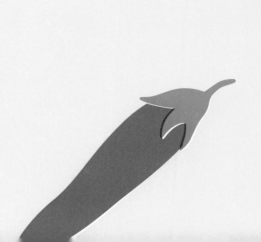

Chilli Crisp Oil

MAKES ABOUT 2 CUPS (500 ML)

I must warn you, this will spoil you not only for all other chilli oils, but for all other condiments, really. Give it away to extend the warm hand of friendship, cement relationships and make others deliriously happy if you must. Or keep the lot for yourself and slather it over anything and everything except – maybe – dessert. The choice is yours.

Heat the oil in a medium high-sided, heavy-based saucepan over medium heat and add the spring onions, garlic, cinnamon and star anise. Bring to a gentle simmer then continue to cook, reducing the heat as necessary and stirring or swirling the pan occasionally, for 20–25 minutes or until the garlic and spring onion are browned and crisp.

Meanwhile, mix the ginger, chilli flakes, soy sauce, smoked paprika and sugar together in a medium bowl.

Strain the spring onion mixture through a sieve into the ginger mixture. Set the garlic and spring onion aside for 10 minutes to cool in the sieve (and allow them to crisp up further), then add them to the chilli oil and give everything a really good stir. Pour into clean jars, seal well and away you go. The oil will keep in the fridge for up to 1 month.

- 1½ cups (375 ml) vegetable oil
- 4 spring onions (scallions), thinly sliced
- 2 garlic bulbs, separated into cloves, then peeled and thinly sliced
- 2 cinnamon sticks
- 4 star anise pods
- 1 thumb-sized (5 cm/2 inch) piece of fresh ginger, very finely chopped
- 3 tablespoons chilli flakes
- 2 tablespoons soy sauce
- 2 teaspoons smoked paprika
- 2 teaspoons caster (superfine) sugar

Sweet Chilli Sauce

½ cup (125 ml) rice wine vinegar

1 cup (250 ml) water

1 cup (225 g) white sugar

1 tablespoon sake (dry rice wine)

1 cup (115 g) finely chopped long red chillies/cayenne peppers, seeds included

½ clove finely grated garlic

1 teaspoon finely grated fresh ginger

1 teaspoon soy sauce

1 tablespoon cornflour (cornstarch) mixed with 2 tablespoons cold water to form a slurry

MAKES 1 X 250 ML (9 FL OZ) BOTTLE

Dipping a spring roll into store-bought sweet chilli sauce is a delightfully saccharine song for your palate to sing, yes, but I do feel a little annoyed by the shameless lack of *chilli* in most sweet 'chilli' sauces. Like, c'mon! So I've perfected a super-quick sweet chilli sauce that actually kicks your ass a bit, depending on how much chilli you wanna use. If it doesn't make you woof a couple of times, maybe you need to add more next time ...

First sterilise your jar or bottle. For some people just those words are enough to make them slam a cookbook shut, but it's easy. Sterilising is as simple as sticking the glass jars or bottles and their lids (unless the lids are plastic) in the oven, turning it to 120°C (235°F), and leaving them for 20 minutes. They're ready to use right away but probably hot, so be careful.

Combine everything except the cornflour slurry in a small saucepan over medium heat and bring to the boil, stirring to dissolve the sugar. Add the cornflour slurry and stir until thickened and glossy (but bear in mind that it will thicken a little more once cooled). Pour into the sterilised jar or bottle and store in the fridge for up to 6 months.

Variations

✳ Serving it freshly made? It's delicious with chopped coriander (cilantro) and a squeeze of lime juice added.

✳ The chilli sauce in my supermarket is literally 50 per cent sugar. (I checked. It says it on the bottle.) The amount in this recipe seems like a lot, but you're allowed to enjoy life and have a bit of sugar. That said – taste it. You might like it with less. It won't keep as long, but your hot ass might.

✳ Fishy chilli sauce: If you love fish sauce, add 1 tablespoon of it to the cooking pot.

TiPS

1 This recipe is easy to scale up if you want to make a huge batch and get a bottling station going. I particularly love chilli sauce as gifts because it's so much better than the bought stuff; if the climate is right, real chillies are something that a lot of lousy gardeners like me can grow successfully; and all the ingredients are cheap.

2 Chilli flakes can vary immensely in hotness, so taste as you go and remember that you can always add more but it's impossible to take it out once it's in.

Bacon Jam

MAKES ABOUT 500 G (1 LB 2 OZ)

Some of you may be horrified by the very thought of this – as Yumi is – but I know enough of you will be thrilled at the idea of making it. I mean, bacon jam! What more could you possibly want?

In truth, this is more like a chutney or relish than a jam – sweet but also tart and intensely savoury. Whether slathered over burgers, tucked into cheese jaffles or stirred into a bolognese, it's a fantastic way to crowbar some life and sparkle back into your everyday dinner game, and it definitely takes those lifesaving quesadillas on page 41 to the next level. Make double and give the excess away, then go about making some bacon jam converts. We could start a cult.

Set a large saucepan over medium heat and add the bacon. Cook, stirring frequently, for 3–4 minutes, until the bacon is starting to crisp and the fat has begun to melt away and render out. Using a slotted spoon or spatula, remove the bacon from the pan and set aside on a plate.

Add the onion to the pan and fry in the bacon fat for 8 minutes, or until it's starting to soften. Add the garlic and cook, stirring frequently, for a further 1 minute, then return the bacon to the pan together with the remaining ingredients. Bring to the boil, then reduce the heat to low and simmer gently, stirring occasionally, for 45 minutes, until the mixture has thickened and reduced, looks shiny and glossy, and smells (and tastes) incredible.

Remove from the heat and leave to cool, then transfer to a clean airtight container or jar. It will keep in the fridge for up to 10 days (although good luck still having any left by then) or in the freezer for up to 3 months.

Nope. — Yumi

500 g (1 lb 2 oz) smoked streaky bacon, thinly sliced
1 red onion, finely chopped
4 garlic cloves, finely chopped
50 g (1¾ oz) soft brown sugar
2½ tablespoons maple syrup
2½ tablespoons apple cider vinegar
1 cup (250 ml) freshly brewed coffee

1 While the jam is simmering, you need to be careful that the bacon doesn't catch in all the caramelising sugars, so be sure to keep a close eye on it and give it a good regular stir as you go. And if it looks like it's getting dry, add a splash or two of boiling water.

2 The coffee is important to give the jam a lovely depth of flavour and provide a bitter counterpoint to all that savoury and sweetness. What coffee you use, however, is up to you – your favourite single-estate bean or instant will do the job equally well.

3 If you wanted to get fancy, this jam makes a great topping for pan-fried scallops.

Perfect Pesto

1 garlic clove (must be fresh)

salt and pepper

1 large bunch of basil

2 cups (90 g) baby rocket (arugula)

120 g (4½ oz) parmesan cheese

⅔ cup (100 g) pine nuts

about ½ cup (125 ml)
good-quality olive oil

MAKES 1 X 350 ML (12 FL OZ) JAR

All pesto is perfect. As a starting point, you want basil – lots and lots of basil. And then you also want cheese, and garlic, olive oil and some sort of nut. It no longer has to be a pine nut but why not? The thing about pesto is that it just can't be faked. There's no mistaking the unique, verdant aroma of the crushed basil leaves, a smell that reminds us we're all creatures existing on a living planet with lives that, like that of a basil plant, are only a short (and hopefully glorious) season. Eating pesto is a way to celebrate being alive.

Smash up the garlic with a large pinch of salt using a mortar and pestle. Scrape it into the food processor, then add all the other ingredients (I would cut up the cheese a bit to give it a head start, and give the pine nuts the quickest light toasting under a warmed grill, taking care not to burn them).

Use a rubber spatula to scrape down the sides of the food processor, process again, then taste, adding more salt or pepper and possibly more oil, if necessary, for an oozy, saucy consistency. (It's impossible to be exact with this recipe because every bunch of basil will be different. Suffice to say, it's also hard to muck up something so simple that's made up of all good things.)

Serve your pesto with freshly made Ricotta Gnocchi (page 153) for the ultimate indulgence – or with any other pasta, as part of a charcuterie board or just on crackers. To store, smoosh it into a jar so there are no air bubbles, and cover the surface with more olive oil. Seal and store in the fridge for up to 3 months. Once opened, use within 7 days.

Dulce de Leche

MAKES ABOUT 800 G (1 LB 12 OZ)

2 x 395 g tins sweetened
   condensed milk

This thick, creamy, perfectly sweet and insanely delicious caramel concoction has been rescuing Argentinians from the dreaded afternoon slump for yonks, but its milky caramel goodness has only recently caught on outside South America. It's incredibly easy to make. Whip it up in bulk and use it in layered cakes, over sundaes, in cookies and as the base for a Banoffee Pie (page 188).

Try to use tins without the easy-open pop tops, and be sure to keep topping up the water as you go – the last thing you want is for the pan to boil dry, the pressure in the tins to build up and your kitchen to end up covered in molten caramel. It's not a good look – or particularly safe.

Remove the labels from the condensed milk tins and place the tins in a large saucepan. Fill with water to 5 cm (2 inches) above the tops of the tins.

Bring to the boil over medium–low heat, then reduce the heat to low and simmer for 2–3 hours, making sure you keep adding water as necessary to keep the tins fully submerged. (The exact cooking time depends on how you like your dulce de leche – 2 hours will give you a lighter caramelisation while 3 hours will give you a deeper, nuttier caramel.)

Remove the saucepan from the heat, then carefully remove the tins from the water and leave them to cool before opening. The dulce de leche will then be ready to use, but if you're piping it or need the texture to be totally uniform, then transfer it to a bowl and whisk well before using.

The dulce de leche will keep for 2 weeks in an airtight container in the fridge or up to 3 months if left in the unopened can in the fridge.

TIPS

1. Like many of the recipes in this chapter, this makes an excellent gift. No one likes a plain tin though, so be sure to whip up a snazzy new label giving some details of what's inside (just make sure you spell it right), and include some suggested uses for all that lovely caramel before you pass it on to the lucky recipient.

2. This recipe is incredibly easy to scale up – just add more tins to the water and use a bigger pan. Condensed milk is one of those odd ingredients that I rarely buy unless I see it on special at the supermarket. It lasts forever, so if you see it at a good price, grab it and keep it in the pantry until you're ready to make this up in bulk.

Ruby Marmalade

MAKES 6–7 X 200 ML (7 FL OZ) JARS

1.5 kg (3 lb 5 oz) mixture of
  ruby grapefruit and blood oranges,
  washed

1.2 kg (2 lb 10 oz) sugar

3 tablespoons agar-agar powder

Is there a more satisfying sound than the *pop* of a jar of home-made marmalade being opened for the first time? Or a better smell than blood oranges and ruby red grapefruit, and their sweet, bitter skins? And one more sensory element hovers over a jar of this marmalade like a sexy rainbow – the look of fruit suspended in reddish-orange jelly, just asking to be smeared on a cracker, scone or bagel, or spooned directly into the mouth. Y.U.M.

I've spent years down the rabbit hole of preserves, jams and marmalades, and let me tell you, people can lose whole weeks to making a marmalade. Me? I'm happy with a recipe I can kick in the dick in under 2 hours. (Disclaimer: there's overnight soaking.)

Cut up the fruit so that the rinds form attractive 3 cm (1¼ inch) long strips about 4 mm (³⁄₁₆ inch) wide. (Don't overthink this though – a lot of them are going to end up as moosh.) Remove any seeds and excessively pithy chunks, then dump the whole lot in a large bowl or the saucepan you'll be using, and cover with enough water to submerge the fruit (this is as much water as you'll need for this recipe). Pop on a lid and leave it stove-side to soak overnight.

The next day, transfer the fruit and water to a large saucepan, stockpot or jam pan over medium heat. As soon as the marmalade starts to boil, turn down the heat so it's cooking at a gentle simmer, then set a timer for 40 minutes. While it's cooking, sterilise 4–6 jars (see page 208).

When the time is up, add the sugar, stirring well to ensure all the sugar has dissolved. Boil gently for another 40 minutes. Now you have to keep an eye on it, stirring frequently to ensure the fruit doesn't stick to the bottom and watching that the pot doesn't boil over. (At this point, preserving purists check to see if the marmalade will set, but the agar-agar powder will mean it absolutely does set. At this stage I would check that you like the flavour and think it's concentrated enough.) Stir in the agar-agar powder, then remove from the heat.

Arrange the sterilised jars in the sink (to catch any drips or spills with minimal mess), then ladle the marmalade into the jars. (I like to do this while the marmalade is fairly hot, as it's more hygienic.) Put the lids on immediately, screwing them on as tightly as you can, then wipe or wash the jars clean. Allow them to cool to room temperature before labelling them and storing them in the fridge until needed. They should last for 3 months.

Blood Plum Jam

MAKES 4–6 X 250 ML (9 FL OZ) JARS

The seasons roll around, and with them the impulse to violently make out with a mango, dig up the garden, preserve things, inhale the smells of the produce and get a big jam-making station going. Years of surveying have me confident that the best of all the jams is blood plum.

Blood plums in and of themselves are the vampires of stone fruit – unnecessarily glamorous, dripping with sensuality and ... well, *rich*. Turning them into jam is a way to enjoy this very seasonal fruit all year round, but the sourness of the skin provides a tartness that can match the sweetness of the sugar required to make this a preserve. And the deep blood colour is a welcome and glorious luxury.

Sterilise 4–6 jars (see page 208) and keep them in the oven until you're ready to use them.

Chop the plum flesh off the stones. Don't overthink it or fuss – no one will ever know if you don't make wonderfully neat quarters with the fruit or if there's a bunch of sloppy asymmetry. Sloppy is what we're going for.

Heat the plums in a large saucepan, stockpot or jam pan over medium heat, stirring from the deep bottom to keep the heat circulating. They will release water/juice and the mixture will become quite wet. Bring it to the boil, then cook at a gentle rolling simmer for 20 minutes. Add the sugar and mix with a large wooden spoon. Add the lemon juice, return to the boil and cook for another 20 minutes. Your jam should be ready now.

If you want, you can use a hand-held blender to whiz up any lumps and pulverise the skins but if you don't, it will be fine. If you're not convinced the jam is thick enough, cook it for another 10 minutes, stirring and keeping an eye on it. You can check it by chilling some saucers in the freezer, blobbing some jam onto a saucer and running your finger through it. If it leaves a line, the jam is done. (I find this step painfully tedious but if I want validation that the jam is good, I might run the blob test on the lid of a container of ice cream or anything else flat that lives inside the freezer.)

Carefully arrange the still-hot sterilised jars in the sink (to catch any drips or spills with minimal mess). Use a milk frothing jug or ladle to scoop jam out of the pot and pour it into the sterilised jars. Put the lids on immediately, screwing them on as tightly as you can, then wipe or wash the jars clean. Set aside until cool, then affix groovy labels, and give them to friends.

The jam should last unopened in the pantry for 2 months, but will grow fur once opened if not stored in the fridge. If you want it to last longer, store unopened up the back of the fridge for up to 6 months. But don't forget to eat it. Before you know it the next blood plum season will be upon us.

1 kg (2 lb 4 oz) blood plums, washed, halved and stones removed

800 g (1 lb 12 oz) sugar

juice of 1 lemon

Quick-pickled Red Onions

MAKES 500 G (1 LB 2 OZ)

3 red onions

300 ml (10½ oz) apple cider vinegar

2 tablespoons caster (superfine) sugar

1 tablespoon salt

6 coriander seeds (optional)

6 black peppercorns (optional)

These colourful spiced sweet and sour onions are super simple to make, are pretty to look at and bring a pop of tangy flavour that will liven up everything from your favourite curry or Mexican dishes to burgers and potato salad. Think of them like jewels and scatter them accordingly.

Peel the onions, then chop them in half and slice them finely.

Pour the vinegar into a saucepan and add the sugar, salt and spices, if using. Bring to a simmer and let it bubble away for 1 minute, stirring, until the sugar and salt have fully dissolved.

Place the onions in a suitable non-reactive container or glass jar. Pour over the warm vinegar mixture, mix together thoroughly, seal well and leave to pickle for 2 hours.

To serve, strain the amount you need from the pickling juice. The onions will keep for 2–3 weeks in the fridge with their pickling juice.

1. The spices here are entirely optional but give the onions a little something extra. To take them in a different direction, try adding 1–2 teaspoons chopped dill and replacing the coriander seeds with caraway seeds for a Nordic vibe; or for a more Mexican style, add a sprinkling of cumin seeds and a thinly sliced fresh jalapeño chilli to the mix.

2. I like these onions because they still have a bit of bite to them, but if you prefer things a bit more mellow, give them a blanch first before using. Simply boil the kettle, place the raw onions in a sieve over the sink, pour the hot water slowly and evenly over them, and let them drain before combining them with the pickling liquid and proceeding as before.

Yoshiko's Tsukemono

MAKES 1 X 500 ML (17 FL OZ) JAR

My mum Yoshiko has a bunch of Japanese friends who hang out at her house, making each other laugh and gambling tiny amounts of cash on their weekly games of mahjong. These gatherings are great, because all these wizened old Japanese people bring over their signature dishes. On mahjong night at Yoshiko's, some of the best Japanese food in the country gets served up to a very select few.

Never really one to big-note herself, Yoshiko said to me recently with twinkling eyes, 'My friends say my tsukemono [pickles] are the best in the world!' I twinkled right back and said, 'Hot damn, they're going in the book.' (Pictured page 36.)

Find a non-reactive pot or container that all the cabbage will fit into, and a plate that fits inside the pot to squash the cabbage down. I use a Pyrex jug and a random royal wedding plate. It doesn't have to be a perfect fit.

Trim off the root and hard parts of the cabbage, and chuck 'em in the compost. Wash the dirt off the outer leaves. Cut the cabbage into 2 cm (¾ inch) slices and transfer to a large bowl. Sprinkle the salt over the cabbage then toss well.

Mix the vinegar and honey together in a small bowl, then pour over the cabbage and mix well (the best way is with gloved hands).

Tip everything into the pickling pot. Flatten the cabbage down so that it's as tightly compacted as possible, then cover it with the plate that fits, and weigh down the plate with a brick or tinned food, or a mortar or whatever other heavy thing you have lying around. (I use a mortar plus one tin.) The pickles will be ready to eat after 4–5 hours but are fine to be left overnight. They're not improved by a longer pickling time, so don't overdo it.

To serve, take out the amount you want to eat, squeeze the liquid out and place it on a cute dish.

Squeeze out the remaining pickles and store in an airtight container in the fridge for up to 2 weeks.

I like to serve them as part of a bento, as a side with any lunch spread, or as a palate cleanser with dishes such as Japanese Pork Belly in Toffee (page 112) or Onigiri (page 35).

½ Chinese cabbage (wombok; about 800 g/1 lb 12 oz)
1 tablespoon salt
about ⅓ cup (80 ml) white vinegar
1 teaspoon honey

Acknowledgements

A huge thank you to Jane Willson, who has believed in us from day 1. Legend.

Big thanks to Jay Gasser, who, by being a terrible cook, gives us something we adore: a willing student! Thanks also to Steph Coombes and Corey Layton at I Heart Radio.

Thanks to the artist who is Vanessa Austin, chicken enthusiast Cath Muscat for taking such wonderful photos, the inimitable and gifted home economist Theressa Klein, cheerful and unusually tall Brendan Garlick (best name for a cook ever), ridiculously clever designer George Saad, word wrangler extraordinaire Nicola Young, and design manager Sarah Odgers and editorial manager Virginia Birch for keeping us all on track.

And finally, thank you to our fucking families who all need to be fed every fucking day, you ANIMALS (we love you).

Index

Published in 2023 by Murdoch Books, an imprint of Allen & Unwin

Murdoch Books Australia
Cammeraygal Country
83 Alexander Street
Crows Nest NSW 2065
Phone: +61 (0)2 8425 0100
murdochbooks.com.au
info@murdochbooks.com.au

Murdoch Books UK
Ormond House
26–27 Boswell Street
London WC1N 3JZ
Phone: +44 (0) 20 8785 5995
murdochbooks.co.uk
info@murdochbooks.co.uk

For corporate orders and custom publishing,
contact our business development team at
salesenquiries@murdochbooks.com.au

Publisher: Jane Willson
Editorial Manager: Virginia Birch
Design Manager: Sarah Odgers
Designer and illustrator: George Saad
Editor: Nicola Young
Photographer: Cath Muscat
Stylist: Vanessa Austin
Home economists: Theressa Klein,
    Brendan Garlick
Production Director: Lou Playfair

*Murdoch Books acknowledges the Traditional
Owners of the Country on which we live and
work. We pay our respects to all Aboriginal and
Torres Strait Islander Elders, past and present.*

ISBN 978 1 92261 671 5

A catalogue record for this
book is available from the
National Library of Australia

A catalogue record for this book is available from
the British Library

Colour reproduction by Splitting Image Colour
Studio Pty Ltd, Wantirna, Victoria
Printed by Hang Tai Printing Company Limited,
China

OVEN GUIDE: You may find cooking times vary
depending on the oven you are using. For fan-
forced ovens, as a general rule, set the oven
temperature to 20°C (35°F) lower than indicated
in the recipe.

TABLESPOON MEASURES: We have used
20 ml (4 teaspoon) tablespoon measures.
If you are using a 15 ml (3 teaspoon)
tablespoon add an extra teaspoon of the
ingredient for each tablespoon specified.

10 9 8 7 6 5 4 3 2 1